GUESTS OF GOD

GUESTS
OF
GOD
Meditations for the Lord's Supper

by
JOHN FREDERICK JANSEN

PHILADELPHIA
THE WESTMINSTER PRESS

Library of Congress Catalog Card Number: 56–8420

ACKNOWLEDGMENTS

Grateful acknowledgment is made for permission to quote from the following:

Basic Convictions, by William Temple. Harper & Brothers, 1936.

Bible: A New Translation, The, by James Moffatt. Copyright, 1922, 1935, 1950, by Harper & Brothers. Used by permission.

Christian Doctrine, by J. S. Whale. Cambridge University Press.

"The Cross Was His Own," author unknown, from *Christ and the Fine Arts*, by Cynthia Pearl Maus. Harper & Brothers. Used by permission.

Cruciality of the Cross, The, by P. T. Forsyth. Independent Press, Limited, London.

"Each one looked inward," from "The Last Supper," by Helen Welshimer. Used by permission of P. H. Welshimer, First Christian Church, Canton, Ohio.

Exposition on I Corinthians, by John Short, in *The Interpreter's Bible*, Volume 10. Abingdon Press.

"Fear wist not to evade," from "The Hound of Heaven," by Francis Thompson, in *Poetry of the Transition, 1850–1914*. The Newman Press, 1936. Used by permission.

Food for the Fed Up, by G. A. Studdert-Kennedy (American title, *I Believe*). Harper & Brothers.

"If He could speak, that victim torn and bleeding," from "The Suffering God," in *Sorrows of God*, by G. A. Studdert-Kennedy. Copyright by Harper & Brothers. Used by permission.

"In Him shall true hearts everywhere," from "No East or West," in *Selected Poems of John Oxenham*. Copyrighted by Erica Oxenham. Used by permission of Harper & Brothers.

Jesus Christ the Son of God, by W. M. MacGregor. T. & T. Clark, Edinburgh, 1907.

"Jesus of the Scars," by Edward Shillito, from *Readings in St. John's Gospel*, by William Temple. Macmillan and Company, Ltd., 1945.

"Jesus shut within a Book," by E. Sinclair Hertel, quoted by

7

Halford E. Luccock in *The Acts of the Apostles*. Harper & Brothers. Used by permission.

"Let Thy Blood in Mercy Poured," by John Brownlie. Used by permission of Marshall, Morgan & Scott, Ltd., London.

Letters to Young Churches, by J. B. Phillips. The Macmillan Company, 1948. Used by permission of the publisher.

Luther's Larger Catechism, translated by J. N. Lenker. Augsburg Publishing House. Used by permission.

Man Born to Be King, The, by Dorothy L. Sayers. Copyright, 1943, by Dorothy L. Sayers.

Meaning of Revelation, The, by H. Richard Niebuhr. The Macmillan Company, 1941. Used by permission.

"O world invisible," from "In No Strange Land," by Francis Thompson, in *Poetry of the Transition, 1850–1914*. The Newman Press, 1936. Used by permission.

"One Bread, one Cup," from "Lord Jesus Christ, We Humbly Pray," by Henry E. Jacobs, in the *Common Service Book of the Lutheran Church in America*, 1917. Used by permission of The United Lutheran Church in America.

Our Faith, by Emil Brunner. Charles Scribner's Sons, 1936.

Pages from an Oxford Diary, by P. E. More. Princeton University Press, 1937.

Poems X and XII, from *Last Poems*, by A. E. Housman. Copyright, 1922, by Henry Holt and Company. Copyright, 1950, by Barclays Ban, Ltd. Used by permission of the publishers. British and Canadian permission from The Society of Authors and Messrs. Jonathan Cape, Ltd.

"Stark cross, above the gray, Judean hill," from *Gates of Brass*, by Donald R. Fletcher. Presbyterian Press, 1942. Used by permission of the author.

What a Man Can Believe, by James D. Smart. The Westminster Press, 1943.

Wicket Gate, The, by G. A. Studdert-Kennedy. Harper & Brothers, 1929.

"Wooden cross," from *Gates of Brass*, by Donald R. Fletcher. Presbyterian Press, 1942. Used by permission of the author.

In Loving Memory
MARY'S MOTHER AND MINE
" Invited to the . . . Supper of the Lamb "
December 4, 1955

CONTENTS

Self-examination

PREFACE

It has been said that the measure of our Christian theology is our view of Christ, and the measure of our view of Christ is our worship in the sacraments. At any rate, parishioner and student alike express a lively interest in finding a more meaningful sacramental observance. A number of recent volumes testify to a rekindled concern today in the sacrament of the Lord's Supper. The present volume does not aim to be an introduction to the Lord's Supper. It is simply and solely a book of Communion meditations.

A few presuppositions have guided these studies. First of all, it is taken for granted that the Supper itself is the "text." Communion meditations serve only to point up and illustrate what the Supper itself speaks. This will explain the choice of Scripture passages. They are chosen for their pictorial quality — appealing, as they all do, to the senses of touch and taste. No suggestion is made that these passages are necessarily Communion texts in a strict sense; some of them are, but others manifestly are not. However, if the Supper itself is the text, these pictures can legitimately serve as parables. In the case of the resurrection narratives, however, the relationship seems stronger to me. I am convinced that these can help us to appreciate what is meant by the Real Presence in the Supper. Too often we have associated the Supper exclusively with the Passion narratives, and have been prone to confuse "communion" with "memorial." In my own parish experience, I loved the custom of having Communion on the Sunday following Easter.

Other illustrative materials are drawn mainly from the hymnals. The Christian of every age finds that the creed that he can sing is the creed by which he can live. Moreover, the hymns have their own way of drawing us to the upper room. "When they had sung a hymn, they went out to the Mount of Olives."

"THE GRACE OF THE LORD JESUS CHRIST"

1

GUESTS OF GOD

"Why does your teacher eat with publicans and sinners?"
MATT. 9:11

A STRANGE question for Communion — or is it? After all, it is a relevant question: " Who are we? "; and it implies a further question: " What are we doing here? "

Jesus had just chosen a disciple, and Capernaum might well wonder at his choice. Instead of consulting the social register or the advice of religious leaders, he had picked Matthew, whom the community had ostracized and who therefore had been living in the shadows of his own loneliness. It was a strange choice. Was Jesus trying to show that God's love reaches out to the unlovely? Was he rebuking the self-righteous complacency of respectable religion? Had he seen through Matthew's callous exterior to the aching hunger of his soul? One wonders how often Matthew had listened to Jesus, and how often he had been on the brink of decision. " Restless is our heart until it finds its rest in Thee."

Well, it was a strange beginning. What follows caused more surprise. Matthew prepared a dinner and invited a host of his erstwhile cronies, a motley crowd of charlatans and outcasts — people like himself, people with a past. He invited them — and Jesus! Doubtless he wished to introduce these friends of the shadow to the light of his new life. Doubtless he wished to commemorate this day of days — " O happy day that fixed my choice! " Whatever the case, the Guest soon becomes the Host,

17

and the supper becomes his supper.

Then the question — curious, critical, upsetting: " Why does your teacher eat with publicans and sinners? ". It is asked by Pharisees of disciples who are too embarrassed to reply. But Jesus hears, and his answer is better than all their poor apologies, for it points immediately to the heart of his gospel: " Those who are well have no need of a physician, but those who are sick."

Come now to another supper — the Lord's Supper. After all, it occasions the same kind of question, and it speaks a similar answer. Why does the Master eat with sinners? Why, indeed? Critics of Christianity love to point to the shames and shortcomings of the Church, and hesitant disciples are still embarrassed to reply. Happily, Christ still answers for those who have no adequate answer, and his answer is here in the sacrament of his love.

Why does the Master eat with sinners? This Supper is not for the proud and complacent. Those who think that they are good enough will always find this table a stumbling block. This Supper is for sinners only. It tells me what I am. It makes me look at myself as he looks at me. Am I really very different from Matthew? Have I not also cheated — God? Why, then, should Christ take time for me?

Yet still he calls, " Follow me." He calls me out of the failures and broken promises of yesterday, promising that if I will come as I am, he will make me what I ought to be.

> " Just as I am! Thou wilt receive,
> Wilt welcome, pardon, cleanse, relieve;
> Because Thy promise I believe,
> O Lamb of God, I come! "

Here in the Supper I may welcome my Lord, I may pledge my faith, and I may join his friends. Paradoxically, however, I soon discover what Matthew found. The Supper becomes far more than my welcome and my dedication. It means infinitely more than what I do " in remembrance " of him. It is his Sup-

per. It is Communion. I do not so much welcome him as he welcomes me. He is the Host who says, " This is my body . . .
for you . . . my blood." This has always been the abiding experience of the Church. Jesus Christ is here — not as our guest,
but as our host. He invites us to be the guests of God, sealing
anew in sacrament what he has done for us in atonement.

> " While all our hearts and all our songs
>   Join to admire the feast,
>   Each of us cries, with thankful tongue,
>   ' Lord! why was I a guest? ' "

If Matthew's feast was a thrilling discovery of fellowship, the
Supper of the Lord is more so. In the Communion, all earth's
isolated and lonely selves are bound together into common
brotherhood and living fellowship. " The bread which we
break," cries the apostle, " is it not a participation in the body
of Christ? We who are many are one body, for we all partake
of the same loaf." In a time that hungers for fellowship and
peace, the Supper of the Lord proclaims the reality of abiding
communion.

Why does the Master eat with sinners? The real force of the
question comes not from the carping critics of the Church. The
real force of the question comes — and ought to come — from
within. As Paul put it: " Let a man examine himself, and so eat
of the bread and drink of the cup. For any one who eats and
drinks without discerning the body eats and drinks judgment
upon himself." The force of that question has made some Christians so uneasy that it has kept them from coming to Communion. Yet it need not keep us away. After all, the question is
asked so that the Lord may reply. His answer is our assurance.
He sups with us because he loves us with the healing love of
God.

It means, you see, that we do belong here. It means that we
may be bold to come here, to find for our restless and burdened
souls the peace of the presence of God. Let us therefore so
come that we may find refreshing and rest unto our souls.

2

"FROM THY RIVEN SIDE"

One of the soldiers pierced his side with a spear, and at once there came out blood and water. He who saw it has borne witness — his testimony is true, and he knows that he tells the truth — that you also may believe.

JOHN 19:34

IT IS characteristic of the Fourth Gospel to notice this detail of the Passion story. Evidently, John sees the spear thrust, not as a historical curiosity, but as a sign of living faith. "He who saw it has borne witness . . . that you also may believe." What does he see?

Some have tried to account for the water and the blood by suggesting that Jesus actually died of a broken, ruptured heart. Not the physical agony of the nails but the mental and emotional agony tore his heart. "He broke his heart, I think, in that last cry," says the centurion of Dorothy Sayers' play *King of Sorrows.*

One may doubt, however, that the Evangelist is trying to give a medical report of Jesus' death. He is bearing witness to the meaning of that death — "that you may believe." What, then, does he see? To be sure, he sees prophecy fulfilled. He sees Jesus, the Lamb of God, slain even as the paschal lambs are being offered. Moreover, he is answering a tendency of his day which questioned the full humanity of Jesus. It really happened, he says. The Son of God died.

However, John sees something more. He sees the whole his-

tory of salvation expressed in the life of Jesus. He sees the cross
not only as an event in the past but as *the* event that shapes the
present. He sees the signs of Jesus' ministry continued in the
life and worship of the Church. Just as all healing and help in
the days of Jesus' ministry found their source in the person of
the Saviour, so all healing and help still derive from Christ.
Above all, he insists, to know Jesus is to enter into the meaning
of his death. From first to last, the cross is always Jesus' hour.
Everything leads up to this hour. Everything derives from this
hour. Accordingly, when John describes the crucifixion, it is
natural that he should see everything drawn into clear and final
focus. In this he is only doing what apostolic witness has always
done — determined " to know nothing among you except Jesus
Christ and him crucified." This is supremely true of Christian
worship, says John. As from the riven side of the Saviour he
sees water and blood flowing, so from the death of Christ he
sees flowing that new life which is shown and sealed in the
sacraments of salvation.

> " Let the water and the blood,
>   From Thy riven side which flowed,
>   Be of sin the double cure,
>   Cleanse me from its guilt and power."

What is a sacrament? It is an unhappy fact that Christians
cannot all agree as to the meaning and number of the sacraments. Two great Christian traditions insist that there are seven
sacraments, which link all the stages of life's pilgrimage to God's
grace. They insist, moreover, that without such sacramental
and priestly mediation the grace of God is not given.

To this, many of us must say no. Sacraments do not add anything to God's Word of gracious love. Rather, they are signs
and seals of that Word, special signs of the love that is already
given. " The sacraments," writes John Whale, " do not add anything to the Word, any more than the kiss and the ring add anything to plighted troth. But they do movingly reiterate it; they
give effect to it."

Moreover, we hold to two sacraments. We do not deny that all of life is sacramental in that it points us to God's handiwork and presence. We do deny that all of life is sacramental in pointing with equal clarity to the saving love of God effected on the cross. Marriage, for example, may be called sacramental in that it points to a "Love divine, all loves excelling," but marriage is not confined to Christian faith, nor does it point to Jesus' death. For that matter, marriage is not given to all Christians. This is why Protestant Christians define as sacraments only those signs given by Jesus himself to all believers, showing and sealing the saving love of God. The two sacraments of Baptism and the Lord's Supper declare that life becomes new, not because of anything we do or can do, but because of Him who makes all things new. Baptism means that life has been made new — so Baptism is not repeated. The Supper means that this new life must continually be sustained and nourished by Him who has made it new, that he who has begun a good work in us "will bring it to completion."

Simply put, the sacraments declare the good news of the gospel — "that you may believe." Once and forever, they declare, Jesus Christ has taken our death and sin so that we may have his life.

> "Draw us to Thy wounded side
> Whence there flowed the healing tide;
> There our sins and sorrows hide."

Said Augustine, "Our sacraments have flowed from Christ's side." So the Evangelist says, "He who saw it has borne witness," and the worship of the Church continues this witness. Think of it! We did this to Christ, but he did this for us!

> "The very spear that pierced His side
> Drew forth the blood to save."

This is as true of Baptism as it is of the Supper. Jesus began his ministry by identifying himself with us in baptism. Significantly, whenever he speaks of his own baptism, he always speaks of his death. " I have a baptism to be baptized with," he says, plainly pointing to his death. That is why Christian Baptism means more than an act of dedication on our part. It declares that long before we ever accepted him, he accepted us and made our life his own.

It is in the communion of the Lord's Supper, however, that we see how the new life is maintained. The wellspring of Christian growth and strength lies, not in external rites however sacramental, nor in resolutions and intentions however noble; it lies in living, continuing fellowship with Christ. " He who eats my flesh and drinks my blood abides in me, and I in him." The Supper declares that Jesus' blood is not only the blood of expiation from past sin; it is also the new blood brotherhood which so unites us with him that we may now be called the children of God. " I have been crucified with Christ; it is no longer I who live, but Christ who lives in me; and the life I now live in the flesh I live by faith in the Son of God, who loved me and gave himself for me."

Thus past, present, and future are linked together in living faith as the whole drama of salvation is brought into the very context of our own experience. With wondering awe and amazement we join the believers of every age as we witness to the wonderful love of God. " He who saw it has borne witness — his testimony is true, and he knows that he tells the truth — that you also may believe." In the sacrament of the Lord's Supper each of us can say, " I do see, I do witness, I do believe."

3

PARADOX AND PROMISE

" I tell you I shall not drink again of this fruit of the vine until that day when I drink it new with you in my Father's kingdom."
MATT. 26:29

THESE are memorable words. One Gospel account of the Lord's Supper begins with these words, and all include them. If Paul does not quote them in his own description of the Supper, he does preserve their thought when he concludes: " For as often as you eat this bread and drink the cup, you proclaim the Lord's death until he comes."

What a strange blending of parting and reunion, of tragedy and triumph, of good-by and good morrow! " I shall not drink again of this fruit of the vine until that day when I drink it new with you in my Father's kingdom." A dirge of death and a rhapsody of resurrection! This is what happens in the cross of Christ, and this is what is shown in the Supper of Christ. Let us examine this double thrust of the Supper.

" I shall not drink again." The words are full of heaviness and dread finality. The end is near. The hour has come. There is no evading or mistaking the somber fact of death. The words come as a shock to disciples, who have been hoping against hope that it would not happen. The words still reject all our attempts to minimize death or to treat evil as illusion. They contrast sharply with some of our funeral customs which often are but piteous and futile attempts to hide the fact of death. We recoil from

the fact of death, writes George Buttrick, because death scores
deep our ignorance and wickedness and finitude.

But not Jesus! He sees death for what it is. He shudders in
Gethsemane, but he does not evade: " My Father, if it be possible, let this cup pass from me; nevertheless, not as I will, but
as thou wilt." In the Early Church there were some who
thought it unworthy and unthinkable that the Son of God
should really die, but the Church labeled such attempts heresy,
and its earliest creed insists that he was "crucified, dead, and
buried." The Church was right. Unless Christ meets us at the
point of our ultimate need, he does not meet us at all. Paul
summed it up in memorable language: " The last enemy . . .
is death." He went on to say that the sting of death is sin, because here everything that makes up life's record is final and
irremediable. " Death has been called the sacrament of sin,"
writes John Whale, " because it is the effective sign of oppor-
tunities gone forever." That is why the death of Christ is the
judgment of the world.

> " Stark cross, above the gray, Judean hill,
>   Against a barren sky, what meaning now
>   Has all life's passing pageantry? You bear
>   The Best that men can ever hope to see,
>   Nailed to your arms, dying. Wooden cross,
>   When He is dead, will not all light be gone?
>   Light, Life, and Hope are gathered round His head
>   That bows in death."
>   — *Donald R. Fletcher.*

" I shall not drink again of this fruit of the vine." A dread
finality lies in these words. If this be all, then we need with
Paul to face the consequences honestly: " If the dead are not
raised, then Christ has not been raised. If Christ has not been
raised, then faith is futile and you are still in your sins. Then
those who have fallen asleep in Christ have perished. If in this
life we who are in Christ have only hope, we are of all men
most to be pitied." Death, the sacrament of sin, allows no eva-

sions. Plato was not wrong in saying that philosophy is the learn-
ing to die.

But we need more. Resignation is not resurrection. Man
needs something beyond a " tragic sense of life." We know that
we must die; that is just our problem. Knowing it, we sense that
there is something more. Let Hamlet epitomize our tragic
dilemma:

> " But that the dread of something after death,
> The undiscover'd country from whose bourn
> No traveler returns, puzzles the will,
> And makes us rather bear those ills we have
> Than fly to others that we know not of."

It is precisely here that Christianity's paradox becomes promise. Here, where sorrow and sin and suffering appear in all their
ultimate reality, here God has come and spoken — in the cross
of Christ. The gospel is the good news that there is Someone
stronger than death, Someone who is able to penetrate the
lostness and separation of our existence so that he can lead us
through with himself. " Who will deliver me from this body of
death? Thanks be to God through Jesus Christ our Lord! "

Yes, thanks be to God. The Last Supper is not really last, for
it is the Lord's Supper. Jesus not only says, " I shall not drink
again of this fruit of the vine." He also says, " Until . . . I
drink it new with you in my Father's kingdom." In the sacrament we do not lament " the touch of a vanished hand, and
the sound of a voice that is still." Rather, we meet Him who
makes all things new. The Supper is not so much memorial as
it is communion. Christ crucified is Christ risen. Thanks be to
God!

Nor shall we end here. The Supper points not only to past
and present; it points also toward tomorrow. " I shall not drink
of this fruit of the vine until that day when I drink it new with
you in my Father's kingdom." " As often as you eat this bread
and drink the cup, you proclaim the Lord's death until he
comes." That day — until he comes! God has a word for life

and history beyond any that we yet have heard. Thy Kingdom come! Christ is the hope of the world as well as the Saviour of men in the world. Paul describes the whole creation as " groaning in travail " for that blessed day. Phillips translates: " The whole creation is on tiptoe to see the wonderful sight of the sons of God coming into their own. The world of creation cannot as yet see Reality, not because it chooses to be blind, but because in God's purpose it has been so limited — yet it has been given hope. And the hope is that in the end the whole of created life will be rescued from the tyranny of change and decay, and have its share in that magnificent liberty which can only belong to the children of God."

As Jesus takes the bread and cup, he sees not only those first disciples, but men of all nations and of all times, joining in communion. His horizon extends until he sees the multitude that no man can number, arrayed in white before the throne of God. So may we.

> " With our sainted ones in glory
>   Seated at our Father's board,
> May the Church that waiteth for Thee
>   Keep love's tie unbroken, Lord."

This is the promise of the Supper. When at Evanston the World Council of Churches was trying to give adequate expression to this Christian hope, John Baillie summed up the theme of the Assembly as " For Kingdom Come and Kingdom Coming." After all, the Christian hope is not the projection of mere desire; it is based on having. Evanston's Assembly rightly saw that, while no theological formulas have adequately expressed this hope, the true index of our having and our hoping is given us in the sacrament of the Lord's Supper. The Assembly's message concluded: " We do not know what is coming to us. But we know who is coming. It is He who meets us every day and who will meet us at the end — Jesus Christ our Lord."

And he is here. He who meets us every day and who will meet us at the end meets us now in the sacrament of his love. He who makes all things new is waiting now to make us new. " Take, eat; this is my body. . . . This is my blood of the covenant. . . . Drink of it, all of you. I tell you I shall not drink again of this fruit of the vine until that day when I drink it new with you in my Father's kingdom."

" The Spirit and the Bride say, ' Come.' And let him who hears say, ' Come.' And let him who is thirsty come, let him who desires take the water of life without price. . . . He who testifies to these things says, ' Surely I am coming soon.' Amen. Come, Lord Jesus! "

4

THE COST OF COMMUNION

" He who comes to me shall not hunger, and he who believes in
me shall never thirst."

JOHN 6:35

" I thirst."
JOHN 19:28

CHRIST crucified, says Paul, is a stumbling block to Jews and folly to Gentiles, but to those who are called, Christ crucified is the power and wisdom of God.

Paul is not exaggerating. The cross is a stumbling block. To spectators, the cross says simply that Christ was not able to do what he promised. He promised life — and the cross is death. He promised victory — and the cross seems defeat. " He saved others," they jeered; " he cannot save himself." To believers, however, the cross speaks of the power and wisdom of God. To them the cross says that life is given only through death, and evil is defeated in the very hour of its triumph. " The weakness of God is stronger than men."

This is vividly illustrated in Jesus' cry, " I thirst." To those who stand outside the circle of faith, that cry seems to say that Jesus has not been able to deliver what he promised. Had he not said that he could give the water of life? Had he not promised that whoever came to him would never thirst? Is he not now admitting his failure? Can he give to others what he does not have himself? Is Christ crucified not a stumbling block? So it has seemed to the spectators.

But " the weakness of God is stronger than men." To those who have been crucified with Christ, the cross speaks rather of the love of God — and love seeks not its own. The message of the cross is that Christ can quench thirst because he himself thirsted, that he can make alive because he himself died.

Love seeks not its own. From the outset of his ministry it was so. In the wilderness Jesus hungered. He swept aside the temptation to avoid that hunger, for it was hunger that linked him with the daily needs of men. He could feed the hungry because he had felt their hunger. " Son though he was, he learned by all he suffered " (Moffatt). Love seeks not its own.

So it was always. He, who lived our life to the full, gives to us what he went without. Weariness is part of the burden of our life. Jesus knew weariness and will stagger under its load, in order that to us he may say, " Come apart and rest awhile." Homelessness is part of the burden of our life, and he had no place where he could lay his head. Yet to us he pledges a Father's home of many rooms. Estrangement is a crushing burden, and Jesus felt its utter dereliction when he cried, " My God, my God, why hast thou forsaken me? " Yet he bore that forsakenness so that we might have his promise, " Lo, I am with you always." Death is the last enemy, and Jesus tasted death for us. " Greater love has no man than this, that a man lay down his life for his friends." Love seeks not its own.

" They borrowed a bed to lay His head
   When Christ the Lord came down;
They borrowed the ass in the mountain pass
   For Him to ride to town;
But the crown that He wore and the cross that He bore
   Were His own —
   The cross was His own.

" He borrowed the bread when the crowd He fed
   On the grassy mountain side,
He borrowed the dish of broken fish
   With which He satisfied;

But the crown that He wore and the cross that He bore
   Were His own —
   The cross was His own.

" He borrowed a ship in which to sit
   To teach the multitude;
He borrowed a nest in which to rest,
   He had never a home so crude;
But the crown that He wore and the cross that He bore
   Were His own —
   The cross was His own.

" He borrowed a room on His way to the tomb,
   The passover lamb to eat;
They borrowed a cave for Him a grave;
   They borrowed a winding sheet;
But the crown that He wore and the cross that He bore
   Were His own —
   The cross was His own."

                         — *Author Unknown.*

" The weakness of God is stronger than men." In the cry, " I thirst," faith hears the gospel of the incarnation. The Word was made flesh. It is no accident that John's Gospel, which most eloquently declares Jesus to be the Son of God, also bears the most insistent witness to his utter humanity.

All this is shown and sealed for us in the communion of the Lord's Supper. Our Lord says to us in this sacrament, " He who believes in me shall never thirst," because he has made our thirst his own. He has come to us — at what cost!

There is a noble page in the Old Testament that relates how David and his stalwarts were hard pressed once in the cave of Adullam, surrounded on all sides by Philistine foes. Adullam was near Bethlehem — so near home, yet so far. In a moment of nostalgic memory David cried out, " O that someone would give me water to drink from the well of Bethlehem which is by the gate! " The wish of their captain became command for three of David's men, who broke through the enemy lines to bring him the water of his desire. And here the story takes a surprising turn. David would not drink of it, insisting that such devotion was proper only to God. We read that he poured it out as an offering to God, exclaiming, "God forbid that I should drink of the blood of the men who went in jeopardy of their lives." The incident is eloquent witness to David's qualities as a leader. He, the captain, was unwilling to quench his thirst at the expense of his men.

A greater than David meets us in communion. He can give us to drink, for this cup is his to give. The Captain of our salvation has known thirst so that he might quench our thirst. Our Captain has himself crossed the enemy lines at bloody cost to bring us the water of life. "He who believes in me shall never thirst." It cost Jesus — Calvary.

And he still thirsts. He yearns for one thing only — that his followers should express their communion with him in lives of love for each other. "Then the King will say to those at his right hand, 'Come, O blessed of my Father, . . . for I was hungry and you gave me food, I was thirsty and you gave me drink. . . . Truly, I say to you, as you did it to one of the least of these my brethren, you did it to me.'"

> "Let Thy Blood in mercy poured,
>   Let Thy gracious Body broken,
>   Be to me, O gracious Lord,
>   Of Thy boundless love the token;
>   Thou didst give Thyself for me,
>   Now I give myself to Thee."

The Gospel says that a soldier gave Jesus a sponge filled with vinegar placed on a spear point. Shall his followers not rather give him the love for which he yearns?

5

TOUCHING THE INTANGIBLE

" Do not hold me."
JOHN 20:17

" Handle me."
LUKE 24:39

T HE reality of Christian worship depends upon the truth of
our Lord's promise, "Lo, I am with you always." This is
especially true of the Lord's Supper if it is to be a communion
and not mere memorial. To be sure, the Supper remembers,
but it does not sigh " for the touch of a vanished hand, and the
sound of a voice that is still." It is communion with a present
Lord.

> " Here, O my Lord, I see Thee face to face,
> Here would I touch and handle things unseen."

This is what the theologians seek to express when they speak
of the Real Presence. It is only when they pass from faith's assurance to explanations that they move from fact to theory — and
dispute.

Perhaps it is better to say simply that we know Christ is here,
we do not know how. Our developed theologies lose too easily
the mystery of faith itself. We want a nice formula — but faith
is content with wonder. Here pictures can help us more than
formulas, for the best commentary on the presence of Christ in
Communion lies in those descriptions of the living Lord found
in the resurrection stories of the Gospels. They do not give us

33

formulas, but they help us " to comprehend with all the saints
what is the breadth and length and height and depth, and to
know the love of Christ which surpasses knowledge."

Well, how does Jesus appear to those who love him? The
stories all have a strangely paradoxical thrust that at first sight
seems contradiction. To Mary, Jesus says, " Touch me not."
To Thomas he says, " Touch me," as to the Twelve he says,
" Handle me, and see." Francis Thompson caught something
of this paradox when he wrote:

> " O world invisible, we view thee,
> O world intangible, we touch thee,
> O world unknowable, we know thee,
> Inapprehensible, we clutch thee! "

Why the paradox? Why does Jesus say to one, " Touch me
not," while to another he says, " Touch me "? Perhaps this
double thrust will illumine the nature of his presence in Communion. Indeed, it is interesting to observe that in Luke's
account, having said, " Handle me," Jesus adds, " Have you
anything here to eat? "

At the outset let us be sure that Christ is neither partial nor
contradictory. When he says to Mary, " Touch me not," he is
not less to her than he is to others. The newer translations
better catch the intent. " Do not hold me," he says. " Cease
clinging to me " (Moffatt).

" Do not hold me." The secret of resurrection life does not
lie in trying to cling to a Jesus of yesterday, but in knowing the
Christ of every day. The New Testament everywhere insists
that Christ's living presence is not less real, but more so, after
the ascension. " Do not hold me," he says to Mary, " for I have
not yet ascended to the Father; but go to my brethren and say
to them, I am ascending to my Father and your Father, to my
God and your God."

Mary needed to learn this, else her love for Jesus would have
become sentimental. All the disciples needed to learn this. In
Dorothy Sayers' *The King Comes to His Own*, Matthew says as

the risen Christ appears, " Why, this is like old times! " But it is not to be like old times again! Christ has come to make old things new.

It is well that we learn this in our observance of the Lord's Supper. Roman Catholic and Protestant Christians alike can cling to Jesus in quite mistaken ways. When the Catholic tries to clutch his presence by supposing that it needs a miracle of transubstantiation which makes the substance of bread into body, when he elevates and adores the elements themselves as the " host," must not Christ say again, " Do not hold me "? Likewise, when the Protestant makes of the Supper a mere memorial that looks back nostalgically to a Jesus of the past, when he tries to recapture the man of Nazareth, must not Christ say again, " Do not hold me "? " Why do you seek the living among the dead? " Is that not clinging to resuscitation instead of reaching out to resurrection? In other words, our ritual can become magical or it can become sentimental, and to both Christ must say, " Do not hold me."

Yet this is but half the story. Do not remove the paradox! Were this all, Christ would remain a stranger, and Christianity would be a cold and forbidding negation of " Touch not; taste not; handle not " (K.J.V.).

" I must be sure," Thomas cries. " I must be sure that the Christ of faith is the Christ of the cross, the Lord I know." " Be sure," Jesus replies. " Put out your hand, and place it in my side." " Be sure," he says to disciples who thought they were seeing a ghost. " See my hands and my feet, that it is I myself. Handle me, and see." " Be sure," he says to us. " This is my body broken for you, and my blood shed. Be sure. It is I myself. Handle me, and see."

" It is I myself." His presence is real, not imagined. In the Supper it is he, not an object or thing, with whom we have to do. As Nathaniel Micklem put it, the efficacy of the Communion " is not in bread but in bread broken." He breaks the bread. He gives himself.

If the Supper and the resurrection both remind us that we

touch the eternal, in another sense they bring us face to face
with historic reality. Our faith rests not on " timeless truth " or
abstract principles, but on historic deed. Sacrament and resurrection alike are anchored in the bedrock of history. It is because the living Christ is the Crucified that we know he is no
stranger to us. Edward Shillito put it movingly in his poem
" Jesus of the Scars ":

> " If when the doors are shut, Thou drawest near,
>   Only reveal those hands, that side of Thine;
> We know today what wounds are, have no fear,
>   Show us Thy scars, we know the countersign.

>   .   .   .   .

> " But to our wounds only God's wounds can speak,
>   And not a god has wounds, but Thou alone."

" He showed them his hands and his side." In a fine passage,
W. M. MacGregor comments: " He said to Mary when she
would have clasped his feet, Touch me not. But Thomas was
invited to touch where the nails had pierced, on which Pascal
makes the comment, ' It is only in His wounds that you can
touch him.' " This is precisely how we touch him in the Supper.
" This is my body broken for you." " It is I myself. Handle me,
and see." Yes, " we must have Thee, O Jesus of the scars."

This is the Real Presence. This is the unfathomable mystery
of divine love. " Do not hold me," Christ says whenever we
are tempted to possess or imprison him within the confines of
our own littleness. But he adds: " See my hands and my feet,
that it is I myself. Handle me, and see."

> " Jesus shut within a Book
>   Is not worth a passing look.

> " Jesus prisoned in a creed
>   Is a fruitless Lord indeed.

> " But Jesus in the hearts of men
>   Show His tenderness again."

6

"O LOVE THAT WILT NOT LET ME GO"

When he was at table with them, he took the bread and blessed, and broke it, and gave it to them. And their eyes were opened and they recognized him.

LUKE 24:30

THE road from Calvary to Christ is the longest and the shortest journey that any man can take. It is the road from death to life, from despair to faith, from judgment to salvation. The story of these travelers to Emmaus has been re-enacted time and again in our own experience. Not infrequently it has been the story of the Church.

Cleopas and his companion had been followers of Jesus. They had been to Calvary, but they had not found their Christ. "We had hoped that he was the one to redeem Israel." Convinced that Jesus' Kingdom had been a brave but broken dream, what was left for them in Jerusalem or in that upper room of Christian fellowship? All that was left was memories — memories of high hopes and tragic loss. The cross had seen to that. All that was left was to talk about what had happened, for there was no future. All that remained was to turn resolutely away from that sad hill of somber shadows. All that was left was to leave Jerusalem for God knows where. "We had hoped that he was the one to redeem Israel." They had been to the cross, but they had lost their Christ.

This thing still happens. It is possible to visit Calvary with-

out finding Christ. In Dostoevsky's novel, *The Idiot*, Prince
Myshkin sees a friend looking at Holbein's painting of the
crucifixion. " I like looking at that picture," the Prince hears
him mutter. " At that picture! " Myshkin cries. " Why, that picture might make some people lose their faith." " That's what it
is doing," the friend agrees. After all, the cross as such is the
victory of evil and the enthronement of death.

> " Wooden cross,
> When He is dead, will not all light be gone?
> Light, Life, and Hope are gathered round His head
> That bows in death."
> — *Donald R. Fletcher.*

" We had hoped that he was the one "! For many modern
travelers to Emmaus it is all over. Oh, they hang on grimly for
a time, they recite the creeds, but they can only point back " to
the things that have happened." They have admired the
prophet of Nazareth, they have loved his teaching and have
sought to emulate his life, but all the while they have tried to
sustain faith on memories instead of on a living presence. And
Jesus, if he is only an event of yesterday, is powerless to save.
Is it any wonder that many moderns who have begun in the
fellowship of the upper room should leave it at length, and turn
their backs upon Jerusalem, not in defiance but in disillusion?
" We had hoped that he was the one "! The Emmaus road has
many travelers, yet, withal, it is a lonely road.

" While they were talking and discussing together, Jesus
himself drew near and went with them." This is always the glory
of the Christian faith. We turn our backs on Christ and Calvary, but he follows us with the persistence of divine love. We
have been talking about him as though he were dead, only to
discover that he is the same yesterday, today, and forever. We
think he has failed, when it is only we who have failed him.

Even when he comes to us, we fail to recognize him. He is
a stranger to us because " the world is too much with us." Yet
we take no journey so far that he cannot overtake us. " O Love

that wilt not let me go! . . . O Light that followest all my
way! " " Whither shall I go from thy Spirit, or whither shall I
flee from thy presence? . . . Thou searchest out my path and
my lying down, and art acquainted with all my ways."

> " Fear wist not to evade as Love wist to pursue.
>   Still with unhurrying chase
>   And unperturbèd pace,
>   Deliberate speed, majestic instancy,
>   Came on the following Feet,
>   And a Voice above their beat."
> — *Francis Thompson.*

The voice interprets the meaning of the cross: " O foolish men
and slow of heart to believe all that the prophets have spoken!
Was it not necessary that the Christ should suffer these things
and enter into his glory? "

It all became plain to them when he blessed the bread and
broke it and gave it to them. Then their eyes were opened and
they recognized him. Is it not so? We try to bend Jesus to our
wishes, but always he brings us back to his cross. The Church
itself is all too prone to leave Calvary for some Emmaus of its
own seeking, but the Supper calls it back. Emil Brunner writes:
" The Lord surely knew what he was doing when, on that last
night, he said to his disciples, ' This do in remembrance of me.'
Without the sacraments the Church would long ago have dis-
appeared, and with the passing of the Church would have gone
also Christian faith and the Bible. The sacraments are the
divinely given flying buttresses which save the Church from
collapse. In how many of the Churches of today do we not
find the sacraments almost the sole Biblical footing — the only
Biblical element that has been able to withstand the caprices of
the gifted minister who lives by his own wisdom rather than
from the Scriptures. Even the most audacious minister has not
dared to lay hands on the sacraments. And they are what they
are! "

All too often we have been so absorbed in our own words

and activity that we fail to recognize the Lord, who has something to say to us. In the sacrament, however, he speaks and acts, addressing us through the eye as well as ear. " The sacraments are God's message for the eye, for the whole body," concludes Dr. Brunner. " One eats and drinks, the whole man partakes of the sacrament. It is, however, not eating and drinking alone, but surely solely and simply permitting God to say what he wants to impart to us, which is just nothing but the gospel, laid hold upon at its heart in the message of the cross. To receive and embrace God's Word in the Sacrament, this alone matters. God acts upon us in the Lord's Supper." The Word is made flesh, and we behold his glory.

One thing more. We read that when they recognized him, he vanished out of their sight. What does that mean? Does it mean that they are left where they were before? Does it mean that even this meeting is one more broken hope? In Dorothy Sayers' play *The King Comes to His Own*, the other disciples ask Cleopas how he can be sure that the whole experience had not been apparition and fancy. His reply is simply, " But the bread *was* broken."

That is enough. We cannot stay at the table, for Christ meets us here so that he may send us out to do his will. The Light of the World does not want us to keep that light in selfish seclusion, but bids us to become the light of the world. In the Supper, then, we do not possess or hold Christ; he possesses us and lays hold upon us. In one sense, then, we ought not to try to " prolong the brief, bright hour of fellowship with Thee." But he *has* met us here. We are not where we were before. " The bread was broken." The tangible presence assures us that Christ lives and will meet us in all the affairs of daily life. It would be quite false to say that the Emmaus story closes with a parting. On the contrary, when they return to Jerusalem, Jesus meets them there. " Hark, my soul, it is the Lord! "

One thing only matters. If ever I have left the upper room of faith or turned my back on the cross, only to discover that Christ follows me with a love that will not let me go, now I can

turn my back on him no more. I cannot stay at Emmaus. I
must return to Jerusalem. The cross which once I fled is now
the magnet of my life.

> "I take, O cross, thy shadow
>   For my abiding place:
> I ask no other sunshine than
>   The sunshine of His face."

7

"LOVING GOD IS . . . LETTING GOD LOVE US"

What shall I render unto the Lord for all his benefits toward me? I will take the cup of salvation, and call upon the name of the Lord.

Ps. 116:12, 13 (K.J.V.)

THIS psalm is intensely personal. Over thirty times the psalmist uses the personal pronoun. He has lately found himself in desperate peril:

"The snares of death encompassed me;
the pangs of Sheol laid hold on me;
I suffered distress and anguish."

He tells us that he was tempted to give up on life, ready almost to conclude that there was no fidelity and no truth:

"I said in my consternation,
'Men are all a vain hope.'"

Instead of despairing, however, he cried out to God, and God answered him.

"For thou hast delivered my soul from death,
my eyes from tears,
my feet from stumbling."

We do not know the nature of his inner crisis, but we know that he came through.

> " When I was brought low, he saved me.
> Return, O my soul, to your rest;
> for the Lord has dealt bountifully with you."

How shall he thank God? " What shall I render unto the Lord for all his benefits toward me? " It is here that he realizes the true nature of faith, and penetrates to the heart of true religion. There is only one way: " I will take the cup of salvation, and call upon the name of the Lord." No one can earn God's love or repay it. As Horace Bushnell put it, " Loving God is but letting God love us."

This is very far from our popular religiosity. Man everywhere has felt the need of God and has called upon God for help, but he does not always acknowledge God as Lord. As long as a man supposes that he can bargain with God, satisfy God, repay God, he is not really meeting God. He may be worshiping a god of his own making, but he is not worshiping the Lord of Hosts. We are inveterate idol makers. We want to be in command of the situation. We want to set the terms of our relationship with God. Our pride is tenacious, even in religion. That is why there is so much legalism in popular religion. In subtle and persistent fashion we try to save ourselves.

" What shall I render unto the Lord? " The experience of a Paul or a Luther is the best commentary upon this question. Paul tried to render God his due. He tried the way of works, the religion of the law, only to discover that the law condemned him. Luther sought earnestly to wrestle his way to inner peace by a fever of activity and penance and prayer. Many try it still.

Why is such religion self-defeating? Why cannot I render God his due? Simply, because as long as I try it, my ego is usurping the throne of God's sovereignty, the finite is trying to dictate to the Infinite, the sinful is trying to placate the Holy. " I find it to be a law," cries Paul, " that when I want to do right, evil lies close at hand."

Faith, however, is something else entirely. Faith means to trust God. Faith means to take God at his word — to believe

that God is gracious. Faith means the end of pride, for it means
to become poor in spirit. "What shall I render unto the Lord
for all his benefits toward me? I will take the cup of salvation."
I will receive his love. I will let God love me. Faith means that
I will let go — to "lay in dust life's glory dead."

> "Not the labors of my hands
> Can fulfill Thy law's demands."

In his engravings on The Book of Job, William Blake expresses this insight vividly. Job's religion had been correct, sin-
cere — but legal and self-centered. Job's God is always drawn
in Job's own image. One of the early engravings, accordingly,
supplements the Biblical picture by showing Job charitably
giving alms to a beggar. However, when God at length has
spoken to Job from the whirlwind, when Job has seen at last
what it means to meet the Almighty, all his proud and correct
religion crumbles. One of the last engravings pictures Job re-
ceiving alms from his friends. To receive when one has been
used to give — that is conversion! "Blessed are the poor in
spirit, for theirs is the kingdom of heaven."

"What shall I render unto the Lord for all his benefits toward me? I will take the cup of salvation and call upon the
name of the Lord." If the psalmist was thinking of the paschal
cup, may we not think of the cup of the Lord's Table? The
Supper forever witnesses to the only way in which we can
render our thanks. "Loving God is but letting God love us."
"See what love the Father has given us. . . . In this is love,
not that we loved God but that he loved us."

If ever we are tempted to make of Christianity a moralism,
the Supper of the Lord reminds us that Christianity is a gospel.
"God so loved the world that he gave." God in Christ has
broken through the shadows, taking upon himself all the hurt
and evil of the world, even its tragic wrongness — for me!
"Thou hast delivered my soul from death, my eyes from tears,
and my feet from stumbling." "Think of it!" cries Paul.
"The Son of God . . . loved me, and gave himself for me"
(K.J.V.). "What language shall I borrow To thank Thee, dear-

est Friend . . . ? " Would it not be rank ingratitude and stub-
born pride and ultimate dereliction to refuse what is so graciously offered? And yet, so long as I try to cling to *my* religion
and *my* pretensions of goodness, I have not clasped the nail-
scarred hand nor received the cup filled with His blood.

Does this mean that what a man does is no matter? Does it
mean that morality is irrelevant or that service is optional? The
psalmist is very far from drawing such conclusions. " I will pay
my vows," he says. I will serve God forever. I will show my
gratitude in my life. Christian faith can never forget this. " By
grace you have been saved through faith . . . not because of
works," says the New Testament; yet, paradoxically, " Faith
apart from works is dead." Faith that has transcended works
bears fruit in works. " The fruit of the Spirit is love, joy, peace,
patience, kindness, goodness, faithfulness, gentleness, self-con-
trol; against such there is no law."

This is true of the Lord's Supper. I do something here. I do
not stand idle. I am not a spectator. " I will take the cup of
salvation." The Supper is not only Christ's seal of grace; it is
also my vow, my pledge, my sacrament. Yet, always, I find my
life by first losing it. I love God best when I let him love me. I
have all when I have surrendered all. " I lay in dust life's glory
dead, And from the ground there blossoms red Life that shall
endless be."

> " Therefore, dear Jesus, since I cannot pay Thee,
>   I do adore Thee, and will ever pray Thee,
>   Think on Thy pity and Thy love unswerving,
>   Not my deserving."

It is only when my life has been emptied of self that it can
become the temple of His presence. " It is no longer I who live,
but Christ who lives in me; and the life I now live in the flesh
I live by faith in the Son of God, who loved me and gave himself for me. I do not nullify the grace of God; for if justifica-
tion were through the law, then Christ died to no purpose."

But he did not die to no purpose! He died for me. " I will
take the cup of salvation, and call upon the name of the Lord."

8

"MY PORTION . . . AND MY CUP"

The Lord is my chosen portion and my cup.
Ps. 16:5

How many of us are sure of God? All yearn for God, but not all have found assurance in God. For many, faith is still a fitful striving for a distant grail. Yet here is a man who can say, "The Lord is my chosen portion and my cup." With Brother Lawrence and the saints of all ages, he has learned the practice of the presence of God, and has entered into the blessed certainty of God's love. He breathes a deeply personal assurance: " Thou are *my* Lord, *my* portion, *my* cup." He has found communion with God. He has tasted the fellowship of kindred minds.

Do not dismiss him as an escapist from reality. He lives in no ivory tower of spiritual detachment; rather, he stands squarely in the history of his time — and ours. He sees not only the reality of a beloved community; he sees also the tragedy of those who foolishly exchange the heritage of faith for the deceptive promises of false gods.

" Those who choose another god multiply their sorrows;
their libations of blood I will not pour out
or take their names upon my lips."

After all, it is always God or gods. " A god," says Luther in his Catechism, " is that to which we look for all good and where we resort for help in every time of need; to have a god is simply to trust and believe in one with our whole heart." Luther continues: " If your faith and confidence are right, then likewise your God is the true God. On the other hand, if your confidence is false, if it is wrong, then you have not the true God." History is the living commentary that " those who choose another god multiply their sorrows." If the gods of Canaan demanded their votive offerings of wine and blood, is it otherwise today? Baal and Bacchus still call for their drink offerings at ruinous cost to body and soul, while Moloch still cries for human blood in war's cruel sacrifice. It is still God or the gods. That is what makes life a solemn choice. " You shall have no other gods before me." " No one can serve two masters. . . . You cannot serve God and mammon." The psalmist knows, and he has made his choice.

What a contrast between God and the gods! The gods demand their libations of blood, but the Lord *is* my chosen portion and my cup. The metaphor suggests the practice of passing food and drink to a guest. God is thus pictured as the Host who freely gives of himself. The man of faith does not need to cringe in fear before some wrathful deity who must be appeased with drink offerings of blood; the man of faith rejoices to find himself the invited guest of a friendly God. God is my chosen portion and my cup. " I have no good apart from thee," the man of faith can say. " Whom have I in heaven but thee? And there is nothing upon earth that I desire besides thee."

> " I keep the Lord always before me;
> because he is at my right hand,
> I shall not be moved."

Such dedication itself becomes a further discovery of God's love. " I keep the Lord always before me " — that is dedication, the realization that God is the transcendent goal of life, surpassing all I know and demanding all I have. Yet this same God is " at my right hand." God is also beside me as the Companion and Friend of my way.

If the psalmist glimpsed this truth, surely the Supper to which
we come speaks more eloquently, for it tells us that the Son of
God has come to stand for us and with us. " The Word became
flesh and dwelt among us." We can be sure of God because
God himself has come to us. " That which was from the beginning, which we have heard, which we have seen with our
eyes, which we have looked upon and touched with our hands,
concerning the word of life — the life was made manifest, and
we saw it, and testify to it, and proclaim to you the eternal life
which was with the Father and was made manifest to us — that
which we have seen and heard we proclaim also to you." This
is the whole message of the Church. As in Browning's poem,
the man of faith realizes that God can only save as God stoops
to where we are:

" 'Tis the weakness in strength, that I cry for! my flesh, that
    I seek
  In the Godhead! I seek and I find it. O Saul, it shall be
  A Face like my face that receives thee; a Man like to me
  Thou shalt love and be loved by, forever: a Hand like this
    hand
  Shall throw open the gates of new life to thee! See the Christ
    stand! "

Even this is not all. Faith not only can say, " God before me
and beside me "; it goes on to say, " God forever." Our psalmist
closes with a glowing intimation of immortality:

" Thou dost show me the path of life;
    in thy presence there is fullness of joy,
    in thy right hand are pleasures for evermore."

" Surely goodness and mercy shall follow me all the days of my
life; and I shall dwell in the house of the Lord forever." All that
I need here and hereafter, cries the psalmist, I have in Him who
shows me the path of life. It is little wonder that Peter should
quote this psalm when he preaches the gospel of the resurrection, for these intimations of immortality become shining cer-

tainty for those who have known Christ and the power of his resurrection. Little wonder that Paul should answer his own question, " Who shall separate us from the love of Christ? " by immediately crying, " Not death! "

> " O in that hour, fairer than daylight dawning,
> Shall rise the glorious thought, I am with Thee."

But come back to today, for the vista of God's endless love is grounded in the present experience of His love. And that love is the love we see on the cross. P. T. Forsyth speaks for all when he writes: " Christ is to us just what his cross is. All that Christ was in heaven or on earth was put into what he did there. And all that man's moral soul needs doing for it eternally was done centrally there. Neither cross nor Christ is simply a historic fact by which we order our mental calendar; they make the sun in our heaven, the force in our world. They make our vital center, not as mere facts, but as sacraments; not because we reckon from them, but because we live from them."

The Table of the Lord expresses movingly that " the Lord is my chosen portion and my cup." Here we meet Him who, instead of demanding impossible votive offerings, offers himself for us. The Lord my cup! " This cup is the new covenant in my blood. . . . This is my blood of the covenant, which is poured out for many for the forgiveness of sins. . . . Drink of it, all of you."

Can I be sure of God? Can my yearning become assurance? The Supper of Christ is answer enough. " The Lord is my chosen portion and my cup."

> " My thirst was quenched, my soul revived,
> And now I live in Him."

9

"A TABLE IN THE WILDERNESS"

Can God spread a table in the wilderness?
Ps. 78:19

THE psalmist has been recapitulating Israel's history as the
history of God's redemptive love despite a people's fickle
faithlessness. He sees as the crowning example the memorable
march through the wilderness. In spite of the miraculous exodus
from Egyptian bondage, in spite of the constant reminders of
God's presence along the way, in spite of all, the people mur-
mured.

> " They tested God in their heart
> by demanding the food they craved.
> They spoke against God, saying,
> ' Can God spread a table in the wilderness?
> He smote the rock so that water gushed out
> and streams overflowed.
> Can he also give bread,
> or provide meat for his people? ' "

Yet the crowning wonder, he goes on, is that God answered
graciously even the question that men asked unbelievingly.

> " Yet he commanded the skies above,
> and opened the doors of heaven;
> and he rained down upon them manna to eat,

> and gave them the grain of heaven.
> Man ate of the bread of angels;
> he sent them food in abundance."

Think of that! Our God meets even our ingratitude and unbelief by opening the very windows of heaven!

Is it too great a leap of imagination from the wilderness of Sinai to the wilderness of today? Surely, if Jesus could use this passage to interpret the meaning of his feeding of the multitude in the lonely wasteland beyond Bethsaida, we may do so again as we approach his Table today.

Ah, wilderness! Now, as then, life has its wilderness journey, for any difficult and untracked region of the spirit is a wilderness way. The wilderness still has its question for which the pilgrim must find answer if he is to find

> " A rest upon the way,
> From the burning of the noontide heat,
> And the burden of the day."

" Can God spread a table in the wilderness? " Well, can he? It is so easy to lose the sense of God's nearness. All of us feel hard pressed at times, and faith has to struggle with the same questions as does doubt, though faith will ask these questions in a different spirit. It does no good to try to stifle such questions, and, happily, God does not ask us to stifle them. He invites us to raise them so that he may answer us at our point of need. " Can God spread a table in the wilderness? " The Table of Christ is answer enough.

Take first the *wilderness of skepticism.* The universe is so vast, its mysteries are so many, its powers are so terrifying, that to many a man the world appears an untracked wilderness. Housman expresses what many have felt:

> " I, a stranger and afraid,
> In a world I never made."

Can such a stranger find home? Can the skeptic find his God? Paul Elmer More, in his *Pages from an Oxford Diary,* tells how he found the way. He had begun as a self-sufficient intellectual, content with the world of ideas, content to search for truth, feeling no need for God or grace. But " an ideal world without a Lord " began to haunt him. " The thought of a naked soul journeying forever on and on through inanimate ideas, with no personal guide or consoler, with no glimpse of the majestic Spirit whose eternal home is there — the thought of such a journey sends a shudder and a chill through me. I cry out: Lord, I believe, help thou mine unbelief! " Then the meaning of the incarnation broke in upon him, the good news that the living God has entered human history in saving and loving personal encounter. Then the professor became a disciple, and the wilderness was wilderness no more. Can we know God? We can and we do, for God has known us and come to us.

Many a disciple has needed such assurance. Thomas cries out for tangible evidence that his faith has not been misplaced. " Unless I see in his hands the print of the nails, and place my finger in the mark of the nails, and place my hand in his side, I will not believe." And Jesus answers Thomas, " Put your finger here, and see my hands; and put out your hand, and place it in my side; do not be faithless, but believing." And Thomas is no longer in a wilderness of doubt. " My Lord and my God! " So in the Supper our Lord speaks to us, not as an object of speculation, but as flesh and blood. " Here, O my Lord, I see Thee face to face."

Again, take the *wilderness of suffering.* Trouble comes to us all, for sorrow and suffering come to saint and sinner alike. " Never morning wore to evening, but some heart did break." The mystery of pain eludes answer, as all of us know. What is there to say in a wilderness of grief? No halting explanations, surely. The heart's cry needs something more than such answers that are not answers at all. " My tears have been my food day and night, while they say to me continually, Where is your God? " Where is God — when you need him? Does he care? Does he know? " Can God spread a table in the wilderness? " He not only can — he has! " Even though I walk through the valley of the shadow of death, . . . thou art with me; . . . thou preparest a table." This is the Christian answer to the problem of pain — not explanations, but the assurance of a divine companionship to see it through. The wilderness of suffering is no untracked wilderness to God, for he has trod it all the way to a hill with a cross. He knows suffering better than we, for he has suffered for us. And he shares our lot still — bearing and sharing, lifting and loving. " Greater love has no man than this "!

" If He could speak, that victim torn and bleeding,
    Caught in His pain and nailed upon the cross,
    Has He to give the comfort souls are needing?
    Could He destroy the bitterness of loss?

.   .   .   .

" Peace does not mean the end of all our striving,
    Joy does not mean the drying of our tears;
    Peace is the power that comes to souls arriving
    Up to the light where God Himself appears.

" Joy is the wine that God is ever pouring
    Into the hearts of those who strive with Him,
    Light'ning their eyes to vision and adoring,
    Strength'ning their arms to warfare glad and grim.

.   .   .   .

" Bread of Thy body give me for my fighting,
    Give me to drink Thy sacred blood for wine,
    While there are wrongs that need me for the righting,
    While there is warfare splendid and divine.

" Give me, for light, the sunshine of Thy sorrow
    Give me, for shelter, shadow of Thy cross,
    Give me to share the glory of Thy morrow,
    Gone from my heart the bitterness of loss."
                                        — G. A. Studdert-Kennedy.

Can we doubt this as we come to the Supper and hear the voice
of Christ say, " This is my body . . . this is my blood "?

Finally, come to the *wilderness of sin*. The deepest jungle of
the spirit is not doubt or pain, but guilt. The peace I need most
goes beyond the mind's assurance and sorrow's comfort; it is
the peace of a pure heart. " The expense of spirit in a waste of
shame," is Shakespeare's description of our moral failures. The
Bible vividly describes this tragic wasteland. Sin transforms the
world from a Garden of Eden to a wilderness of conflicting desires and a tangle of broken purposes. Sin drives the prodigal
from the joy of a father's home to the regions of famine. " O
wretched man that I am, who shall deliver me? " More than
signposts are needed. Is there a way to faith's promised land?
Can God rescue and redeem? Can God spread a table in this
wilderness?

> " Still journeying on amid the waste,
>   And fainting oft beneath the strife,
>   Our longing spirits yearn to taste
>   Thy heavenly food, O Bread of Life!

> " And when our broken cisterns fail,
>   And leave us thirsting on the sod,
>   When all the powers of sin assail,
>   We need thy strength, O Wine of God! "

Here especially the Supper of Christ speaks its healing word:
" Take, eat; this is my body, broken for you. This cup is the new
covenant in my blood, shed for the remission of sins. My peace
I give to you. Your sins are forgiven. Go, and do not sin again."

God does not wait for us to come to him. He has come to us.
He who knew no sin became sin for us. This is the gospel —
not an impossible summons, but a gracious invitation.

Yes, " Thou preparest a table before me." Thanks be to thee,
O God.

10

STRENGTH FOR THE JOURNEY

" Arise and eat, else the journey will be too great for you."
I Kings 19:7

THERE are times when even stout hearts faint and strong men falter. " Even youths shall faint and be weary, and young men shall fall exhausted." When yesterday's victories are buried in today's failures, when tomorrow beckons no hope, when everything appears thwarted by circumstances over which we have no control, when we have lost the certainty that once illumined our way — what then? The Scripture promises that precisely then " they who wait for the Lord shall renew their strength." Is it true?

There was a day in Israel when faith in God was hard pressed. When Jezebel's religion of Baal was calling into question the very foundations of Israel's faith, when everything seemed shaken, Elijah appeared as a fearless prophet of God's righteousness, proclaiming the judgment of God upon history and witnessing to the power of the Almighty. And yesterday, on Mount Carmel, he had dared king and priest in the name of the Lord of Hosts, and had won the victory of faith.

However, the exaltation and triumph of that moment had quickly vanished. The prophet knows that Jezebel's fury has merely redoubled, and yesterday's victory is buried in today's difficulty. " Then he was afraid, and he arose and went for his life."

From the mountain top to the slough of despond! From the shadow of the Almighty to the shade of a broom tree! "He asked that he might die, saying, 'It is enough; now, O Lord, take away my life.'"

> "Sometimes I'm up, sometimes I'm down,
>   Oh, yes, Lord;
> Sometimes I'm almost to de groun,
>   Oh, yes, Lord."

Happily, God has a better way. "And he lay down and slept under a broom tree; and behold, an angel touched him, and said to him, 'Arise and eat.' And he looked, and behold, there was at his head a cake baked on hot stones and a jar of water. And he ate and drank, and lay down again. And the angel of the Lord came again a second time, and touched him, and said, 'Arise and eat, else the journey will be too great for you.' And he arose, and ate and drank, and went in the strength of that food forty days and forty nights to Horeb the mount of God."

A strange and romantic story? But is it more strange and more wonderful than what we find on today's road? Like the prophet of old, many of us have climbed some mount of victory and have shared that exhilarating sense of God's nearness and power. Like him, there have been times when we were so sure of God. But like him also, we have found that one does not stay on the mountain height in unchallenged victory. The task we thought finished we find has only begun. The road we thought ended we find winding suddenly into desert loneliness. Many a man has found himself ready to say: "It is enough, O Lord. I can't take it any more."

In such dark nights of the soul there comes a voice, not of an angel, but of Christ. "Arise and eat, else the journey will be too great for you." We wake from the gloom that has clouded our vision, and we see a table prepared for us. When our own resources have failed us, when our loneliness has oppressed us, we hear the voice of Christ, "Arise and eat." The words contain a promise and they enjoin a task.

Please be patient with me - God hasn't finished yet

The words hold a *promise*. The prophet had fallen prey to abject discouragement because he had come to feel utterly alone. " I, even I only, am left." Such loneliness is a desolating experience, as the Ancient Mariner well knew:

> " O Wedding-Guest! this soul hath been
> Alone on a wide, wide sea!
> So lonely 'twas, that God himself
> Scarce seeméd there to be."

Happily, however, Elijah discovered in the wayside supper the companionship of God. Alone, the journey is too great, but with God's comradeship no journey is too hard. " They who wait for the Lord shall renew their strength." " And he arose, and ate and drank, and went in the strength of that food forty days and forty nights to Horeb the mount of God." In other words, the supper sent him back to the place of memory and heritage — the mount where God had spoken to Moses in convenant love. All of us need to return from time to time to the place of first vision, the mount of God.

This is the message of the Lord's Supper. It tells us that if the road is hard for us, there is One who walked life's road for us. His road led him to embrace all our loneliness and night on a mount called Golgotha. There, in the context of all that evil and death could do, he cried out, " My God, my God, why hast thou forsaken me? " only to know at length that " into thy hands I commit my spirit." He has met loneliness and separation for us. In the Supper we know that we are not alone, for he has led us back with himself to stand in memory at the cross.

The mount of God, however, is more than a place of hallowed memory. It is the scene of communion. Elijah at the mount does not merely remember the God of Moses. He finds that the God of Moses still speaks. So we find that Christ crucified is Christ risen, the Lord and Companion of our way.

Moreover, the promises of God are always made tangible.

Elijah had cried, "Lord, I only am left." God's answer not only assures him that there are seven thousand faithful; God's answer is brought home to him in the friendship of Elisha. So our communion not only binds us to God; it enables us to share in the communion of saints. "Drink of it, all of you," Jesus says, and we find our togetherness in the Supper.

"We, though many," says Paul, "are one body." This is not a theoretical knowledge; it finds concrete expression in the life of each congregation and family and friendship. "Lord, I only am left." Not so! "You are no longer strangers and sojourners, but you are fellow citizens with the saints and members of the household of God."

"Arise and eat, else the journey will be too great for you." Then there *is* a journey — the words contain a *task* as well as a promise. God's grace is not given to free us from service but to equip us for service. The journey led the prophet back to the tumultuous and dangerous arena of his own national life. As he heard the still, small voice at Horeb, he knew there could be no evading the divine summons. "Go, return!" Not in detachment or in withdrawal, but in the warp and woof of his time, must Elijah bear his witness.

The Supper also bespeaks a task. It is not only the seal of God's promises to us; it is also the renewal of our allegiance to him. Christ offers us no escape from the toil and pain and struggle of life. He bids us follow him, telling us that the cross is a condition for discipleship, for the disciple is not greater than his Lord. He will not allow us to tarry in the cleft of the rock, away from the tumult and confusion of our time. When a disciple once tried to persuade Jesus to forget the journey to the cross, he replied, "Get behind me, Satan!"

> "Where cross the crowded ways of life,
>   Where sound the cries of race and clan,
>   Above the noise of selfish strife,
>   We hear Thy voice, O Son of Man.

[0]   •   •   •   •   •   •

> "O Master, from the mountain side,
>   Make haste to heal these hearts of pain;
> Among these restless throngs abide,
>   O tread the city's streets again."

And he can only as he lives in us. "This is my commandment, that you love one another as I have loved you. . . . He who abides in me, and I in him, he it is that bears much fruit, for apart from me you can do nothing. . . . Take, eat, this is my body. . . . Arise, let us go hence."

This is the relevance of the Lord's Supper. It sends us on our way — with him. "O Master, let me walk with Thee."

11

THE KING'S TABLE

So Mephibosheth ate at David's table, like one of the king's sons. II SAM. 9:11

A N OLD page from the Bible has a half-forgotten bit of story that becomes a parable for today.

Here is the story. After the long years of Saul's enmity have done their worst, David's kingdom is at last secure in Jerusalem. The shepherd of Bethlehem is king of Israel now, enjoying the homage of his people and the respect of his foes. Yet David has not forgotten the memories of yesteryear, for his thoughts go back to the covenant he had sworn with Jonathan, Saul's son. Saul is dead now, and Jonathan is dead, but the memory of a blessed friendship and a solemn vow live on. What if some member of that once royal house is still alive, " that I may show him kindness for Jonathan's sake "? And one son of Jonathan is found, the last of a once noble house. A pitiable figure of a man is this Mephibosheth. When the dreadful tidings of the death of Saul and Jonathan in the battle of Gilboa had reached home, a terrified nurse had dropped the child, and Mephibosheth had grown up hopelessly crippled. " He was lame in both his feet." Moreover, family ruin had crippled his spirit, leaving deep scars upon his timid, lonely, helpless soul.

Something welled up in David's great heart when he saw him. Instead of remembering the hostility of Saul's house which had pursued him relentlessly during outlaw days and civil strife, instead of scorning this hesitant, halting man who lacked the winsome strength of his father, David only remembered Jonathan, and he saw something of Jonathan's strong manhood in this wretched figure bowing before him. " As for Mephibosheth," David said, " he shall eat at my table as one of the king's sons." No truant charity was this, but a real adoption. In a day when bitter blood feuds were the accepted order of practical politics, this little bit of story stands apart.

It is a refreshing story. However, if we allow imagination to play upon the scene, it becomes not only a story of the past but a parable that draws us to a greater than David and to a more blesséd Table.

How do we come to the Communion table of our Lord? What happens to us here?

We have no claim here. The painful memory of insurrection separates us, for sin means our kingdom against God's Kingdom, our will against his will. Such insurrection has left its crippling marks upon us. Our attempt to " go it alone " always leads to the shambles of defeat. What burdens of anxiety we carry, what memories of regret and failure haunt us, what multiple handicaps and scars of soul we all bear! " All have sinned and fall short of the glory of God " is the solemn verdict of Scripture. Not only some bitter and violent Saul feels the sting of death on Mount Gilboa. Jonathan dies there too, and, far away, a helpless baby is touched by its defeat. We are all bound together in the bundle of life. Children of God we were meant to be; children of defeat and death we have become.

Dare I come to the table of the rightful King whose dominion I have so long disputed? If Mephibosheth trembled in the presence of David, shall I not tremble in the presence of my Lord? Let a man once stand in the presence of the Holy, and he sees himself for what he is. " Woe is me! For I am lost; . . . for my eyes have seen the King, the Lord of hosts! " Isaiah's cry finds its counterpart in Peter's exclamation, " Depart from me, for I am a sinful man, O Lord." It finds its counterpart in every genuine, penitent cry of man's spirit.

And yet, I come! I come because the King of Glory bids me come. If I have been afraid to come to him, he has come to me. His love has embraced me, not for the sake of some Jonathan dead and gone, but for the sake of Him who triumphantly met the shadows of Calvary, who died and rose again and is alive forever. This is the meaning of the Table of the Lord. This is why I can come.

And what happens here? " He shall always eat at my table . . . like one of the king's sons." David's gracious words to Mephibosheth only begin to suggest the grace of Him who says, " Who are my mother and my brothers? " and who points to those who sat about him, saying, " Here are my mother and my brothers! " This is the good news of God, echoed and re-echoed on every page of the New Testament and on every page of Christian experience. " To all who received him, . . . he gave power to become children of God." Sons of God, adopted into the royal family of heaven — that is Christianity. Listen to Paul's words: " All who follow the leading of God's Spirit are God's own sons. Nor are you meant to relapse into the old slavish attitude of fear — you have been adopted into the very family circle of God and you can say with a full heart, ' Father, my Father.' The Spirit Himself endorses our inward conviction that we really are the children of God. Think what that means."

Yes, think what that means! An exile on the island of Patmos knew what it meant: " To him who loves us and has freed us from our sins by his blood and made us a kingdom, priests to his God and Father, to him be glory and dominion for ever and ever." A Christian man can fling away the fears that have shadowed him, he can cast off the regrets of past failure, he can throw aside the crutches of his weakness, he can walk triumphantly with his Master. He is no exile or stranger — he is a King's son!

> " All I could never be,
> All men ignored in me,
> This I was worth to God."
> — *Robert Browning.*

It still happens. It happens whenever Christ lays his healing and helping hand upon us to lift us above the bondage of the past.

> " Take, my soul, thy full salvation,
>   Rise o'er sin and fears and care;
> Joy to find in every station
>   Something still to do or bear.
> Think what Spirit dwells within thee,
>   What a Father's smile is thine,
> What a Saviour died to win thee:
>   Child of heaven, canst thou repine? "

Take it then — thy full salvation! Take this forgiving grace of God that forgives the rebellions of the past. Take this strong comradeship that receives you into the family of God. Take this love that bids you come and stay forever. " Take, eat, this is my body which is broken for you." " O taste and see that the Lord is good! "

12

THE KING'S CUPBEARER

I was cupbearer to the king.
NEH. 1:11

IN THE annals of patriotism and faith the stirring memoirs of Nehemiah deserve to be remembered. He lived in the Persian capital of Susa, far from the home of his fathers. He had risen to prominence in the court, for he was cupbearer to the king. The title denotes a custom of ancient days that held it a mark of esteem to be able to taste the king's wine — to see if it were poisoned! " I was cupbearer to the king." Then, one day, news comes to Nehemiah from Jerusalem about the desperate and despairing condition of the little Judean colony. He hears how Jerusalem's wall is broken and how the people's spirit is crushed. The news stuns him — and stirs him to action. With diplomatic humility and skill he asks the king's permission to return to Jerusalem and help to rebuild the walls. So begins a noble and stirring chapter in Judah's restoration. " I was the king's cupbearer."

The old story has in it a parable, certainly not intended, yet nonetheless suggestive. Our postwar world of ominous uncertainty and changing culture has some of that mingled sense of disillusion and opportunity that marked Nehemiah's day. Separated as we may be from him in years and miles, Jerusalem is still a name that can arouse our memories and longings, for it speaks of our spiritual heritage. " Jerusalem the golden," the

" sweet and blessed country that eager hearts expect." World history may march on — and we have to march with it — but always there is a tug of memory and a homesickness for a blessed community of God — " beneath thy contemplation sink heart and voice oppressed." And I too would speak with my King concerning the deep longings of my heart. I too may approach my Lord at Supper, for I too am the King's cupbearer.

Yet what a difference! The cupbearer of old must come trembling before some foreign prince in a foreign capital. His king may command or concede, but, withal, he remains regally aloof from the heartaches of a defeated people.

But come to that Supper where you are privileged to be cupbearer, and listen to the words of your King. " The kings of the Gentiles exercise lordship over them; and those in authority over them are called benefactors. But not so with you; rather let the greatest among you become as the youngest, and the leader as one who serves. For which is the greater, one who sits at table, or one who serves? Is it not the one who sits at table? But I am among you as one who serves." And then this King rises from table and takes a towel and begins to wash his servants' feet!

Think what that means! " Though he was in the form of God, [he] did not count equality with God a thing to be grasped, but emptied himself, taking the form of a servant, being born in the likeness of men. And being in human form he humbled himself and became obedient unto death, even death on a cross." This is the astonishing wonder of divine love, that lordship should express itself in lowliness, that sovereignty should manifest itself in sacrifice. The kings of the earth sit at table waiting to be served and honored, proud of being benefactors, but the Christ of God rises from table to wash his servants' feet.

And no foreign king is Jesus. We need go to no foreign court to find him. In the place of our need we touch him who has made our need his own. " He had to be made like his brethren in every respect," says the New Testament. " For because he

himself has suffered and been tempted, he is able to help those
who are tempted." This is the very heart of the evangel, namely,
that God has made common cause with man in the wonder of
incarnate love. "The Word became flesh." The kings of earth
may be called benefactors, but our King is called Saviour and
Friend. "No longer do I call you servants . . . I have called
you friends."

If our King is different, so is his cup. It is not I who must
taste the cup to see if it holds death for the king. It is rather
the King who has already tasted the cup lest I should die. The
cup is the cup of his blood poured out for me. He tasted my
death that I might have his life.

> "Thy body, broken for my sake,
>   My bread from heaven shall be;
> Thy testamental cup I take,
>   And thus remember Thee."

In what sense, then, can I be his cupbearer? "We have this
treasure in earthen vessels, to show that the transcendent power
belongs to God and not to us." Paul says that we may bear
about in the body the dying of the Lord Jesus that the life also
of Jesus may be made manifest in our mortal flesh.

> "When we taste the mystic wine
> Of Thine outpoured blood the sign,
> Fill our hearts with love divine."

This the King's Supper seals for us. This the King's love has
bought for us. Shall I not approach this Supper with glad and
grateful devotion? Am I not the King's cupbearer?

"THE COMMUNION OF SAINTS"

13

THE INEXHAUSTIBLE CHRIST

And all ate and were satisfied.
LUKE 9:17

THE feeding of the five thousand is the only miracle of
Jesus that is recorded in all four Gospels. All see it as a
watershed in the ministry of Jesus. Why did this one story so
grip the imagination of the Evangelists? That they saw it as a
staggering evidence of the power of Jesus is, of course, true
enough; but was it more staggering than raising the dead or
stilling the storm? Evidently this sign had for them some
particular relevance. The Fourth Gospel makes plain what is
latent in the others — this miracle is the sign of what is continually happening in the life and worship of the Church. John
follows the miracle with the long discourse on the Bread of Life,
and he interprets the feeding of the multitude in sacramental
language. And John is right. This page from the Gospels comes
alive with meaning if we see it, not as some unrelated episode of
the past, but as the sign of what the living Christ continues to
do in the Church.

After all, what has the Church to offer the world? How can
the Church deal with the multitude? Some disciples still throw
up their hands, saying that the problems are too many and the
resources too few. "Send the crowd away." We cannot help.
But Jesus will not let his disciples do this. "You give them
something to eat," he says. When disciples reply that they have

only very inadequate resources — what are these among so
many? — he still insists that the crowd's needs be met. He tells
the disciples to make the people sit down. This, at any rate, the
Church can do. It may not be able to meet the world's need,
but it can invite people to come and stay, trusting that the living Christ is able to do what men cannot do.

This is the meaning of the Lord's Supper. The Church can
provide the setting and can bring its small resources — the Lord
of the Church must use them. The hope of the world lies, not
in these few elements of bread and wine, but in Him who is
himself the Bread of Life. He makes this table his Supper, and
he is able to do far more abundantly than all we can ask or
think. And the wonder continues through all the centuries of
Christian experience: " And taking the five loaves and the two
fish he looked up to heaven, and blessed and broke them, and
gave them to the disciples to set before the crowd. And all ate
and were satisfied."

If the physical miracle was staggering, that so many were fed
with what seemed so little, it pales into insignificance beside
a greater miracle. For twenty centuries the living Christ has

been feeding all who have come to him for the Bread of Life,
and no one has yet been sent away hungry who has come in
faith: " For my flesh is food indeed, and my blood is drink indeed." And the wonder still goes on — all eat and are satisfied, and still there is grace enough and to spare.

Picture the varying needs in that crowd of Bethsaida. Picture
the needs represented in any Christian congregation today. Here
is a woman whose heart is nearly broken for a loved one gone.
Yonder is a man burdened with anxiety over some unexpected
reverses. Next is one whose spirit is broken and on whose face
hopelessness is writ large. Here is someone who has been carry-
ing a grudge that is blighting his soul, while another has been
defeated in his battle with temptation. All seek anonymity in
the crowd, but the eyes of Jesus see each one — and each knows
it! What burdens people carry! In that crowd of Bethsaida, as
in any congregation on Sunday morning, there is heartache

behind many an outward smile, and fear behind much outward composure. Always there is a persistent hunger for peace with God, a craving for his pardon and fellowship. " Restless is our heart until it finds its rest in Thee."

The miracle still happens. " All ate and were satisfied." It happens every time that men and women meet with Jesus Christ and find their heart hungers satisfied in his inexhaustible love. It happens in the Lord's Supper. Here, more than ever, people find Christ as the Bread of Life. Here, more than ever, he discloses himself as a very present help in every kind of trouble. When this lonely woman comes to the Supper, she knows that she is not alone. " Thou art with me. . . . Thou preparest a table before me." When the man burdened with anxiety comes, he finds the promise fulfilled: " Let not your heart be troubled; . . . believe . . . in me. . . . My peace I give to you." When the soul that has carried bitterness tastes the love of God, it becomes clear that bitterness must go. " This is my commandment, that you love one another as I have loved you." When anyone who has wrestled with doubt comes, he reaches out with Thomas to touch the nail-pierced hands, and he can cry out in full assurance, " My Lord and my God!" When the man who has been defeated in the battle of his soul comes, he finds that there is Someone beside him who is stronger than temptation, and he can take heart again as he hears a Voice say, " Be of good cheer, I have overcome the world." Every one of them knows that Christ has what he needs. This is the continuing miracle of the inexhaustible love of Christ. " And all ate and were satisfied."

Indeed! " And they took up what was left over, twelve baskets." Enough and to spare! Enough and to share! This we can do — gather the abundance of love to bring it to others. For the Christ who has fed us yearns to feed others also. " I have other sheep, that are not of this fold." The Communion of the Lord's Supper is not an end in itself; it enables us to share with others the inexhaustible love of God. " My God," cries Paul, " will supply every need of yours according to his riches in glory in Christ Jesus," and so Paul spent his life sharing the love he had found.

So the miracle of love continues, until all have eaten and they shall hunger no more, neither thirst any more.

14

OUR CONTINUING COMMUNION

And they devoted themselves to the apostles' teaching and fel-
lowship, to the breaking of bread and the prayers. . . . And all
who believed were together and had all things in common. . . .
And day by day, attending the temple together and breaking
bread in their homes, they partook of food with glad and gener-
ous hearts, praising God and having favor with all the people.
And the Lord added to their number day by day those who were
being saved.

ACTS 2:42, 44, 46, 47

EASTER is no epilogue or happy ending to the life of Jesus. It *is* the life story. The resurrection is not an ending but a be-ginning. Luke expresses this as he opens his second volume, The Acts of the Apostles, by saying, " In the first book . . . I have dealt with all that Jesus *began* to do and teach." He im-plies that now he will describe what Jesus *continues* to do and teach. This is apostolic faith — now is Christ risen! Faith is not reverence for a memory but communion with a Lord.

Why is it, then, that Easter is for so many only a momentary vision and a fleeting glory, rather than an abiding awareness? For a moment Easter faith mounts on eagle wings, but soon, all too soon, the vision is clouded by the anxieties and cares of the day. No wonder that Christians are sometimes nostalgic:

> " Where is the blessedness I knew
> When first I saw the Lord?

Where is the soul-refreshing view
Of Jesus and His Word? "

One cannot but contrast such fleeting assurance with the
resurrection faith of the New Testament. The glory of the
resurrection faith of the first disciples lay in the fact that it
permanently changed their lives. Whereas beforehand we saw
them afraid, fickle, quarrelsome, and powerless, now we watch
them burst upon the scene unafraid, united, and faithful. How
could they be so sure that Christ their Lord was with them?
Why, Christ appeared to them!

How did he appear? Was Easter confined to one day? Was
the resurrection experience limited to a few choice men? Had
such been the case, there would have been no Church and no
ongoing Christianity. After all, you and I are not apostles. The
question is, Can we have what they had?

Happily, Christ did not come in a single, shining glory. "To
them he presented himself alive after his passion by many
proofs, appearing to them during forty days, and speaking of
the kingdom of God." Luke goes on to say, " Staying with
them," or, as the margin reads, " eating " with them. As one
reads the resurrection narratives, one cannot help being struck
by the fact that the risen Lord manifests himself so often in the
breaking of bread. Peter will testify that " God raised him on
the third day and made him manifest . . . to us who were
chosen by God as witnesses, who ate and drank with him after
he rose from the dead." It was as the disciples saw the pierced
hands breaking bread, as they heard the beloved voice giving
thanks, that they knew the resurrection was no fleeting moment
but a continuing communion. Some scholars tend to deplore
this detail in the narratives, dismissing it as an early tendency
to materialize the supernatural. Yet it is this very detail of eating
and drinking that has abiding relevance for us today. How can
we keep Easter faith alive? After all, even for the first disciples,
the forty days are quickly gone. May it not be in this eating and
drinking that we find our continuing communion?

Here, at any rate, is the glorious fact. Others besides those first followers have known Christ and the power of his resurrection. What is the Church? James Smart writes, " The Church is a body of people in whom Jesus Christ himself lives again to work his works, to speak his words, and to feed the souls of men." The communion of saints — the reality of a beloved community — rests upon an unbroken communion with Christ. Here is the description of the Early Church: " They devoted themselves to the apostles' teaching and fellowship, to the breaking of bread and the prayers. . . . And all who believed were together and had all things in common. . . . And day by day, attending the temple together and breaking bread in their homes, they partook of food with glad and generous hearts, praising God and having favor with all the people."

Why should they or we hanker wistfully for the forty days? " Henceforth," cries Paul, " we know not Christ after the flesh, but after the spirit." Essentially we know him the same way. He appeared to them in the breaking of bread, and he appears to us in the breaking of bread. The Acts of the Apostles can be translated into The Acts of Today whenever Jesus Christ himself lives again to work his works, to speak his words, and to feed the souls of men. The risen Lord is still the Jesus of the scars. The living Lord is still the loving Son of Man. This the sacrament told them, and this it tells us. " This is my body . . . my blood. . . . Lo, I am with you always, to the close of the age." No wonder that the New Testament will call Jesus " Alpha and Omega " — the Beginning and the End. He is the same yesterday, today, and forever. We do not live in the afterglow of faith. We too are knit forever to him who is their Lord and ours.

What are the marks of such communion? " All who believed were together and had all things in common. . . . And day by day, attending the temple together and breaking bread in their homes, they partook of food with glad and generous hearts, praising God and having favor with all the people."

Note first the emphasis on *together*. They met, worshiped,

prayed, and ate together. "No man is an island," and a Christian life lived for itself alone is a contradiction in terms. Christianity is communion — the communion of saints grounded in the communion of Christ. "So then you are no longer strangers and sojourners, but you are fellow citizens with the saints and members of the household of God."

> "In Him shall true hearts everywhere
> Their high communion find;
> His service is the golden cord
> Close binding all mankind."

Another mark of such communion is *joy and praise*. "They partook of food with glad and generous hearts." Christ speaks to us in this Supper as he spoke to his first disciples: "These things I have spoken to you, that my joy may be in you, and that your joy may be full." It is the characteristic note of the New Testament: "Rejoice in the Lord always; again I will say, Rejoice." We call the Supper the Eucharist, the Thanksgiving. Let us always partake with glad and generous hearts. "Drink this in remembrance that Christ's blood was shed for thee, and be thankful." One of our hymns reads, "This is the hour of banquet and of song." Here the Supper epitomizes the secret of the Christian life — "Jesus, thou Joy of loving hearts." Yet it is no lighthearted gladness, for our joy was dearly bought.

There is a third mark of true communion: "*Having favor with all the people*." The quality of their lives made others want to become Christian. "How these Christians love one another!" a Roman official wrote in amazement. T. R. Glover said that Christianity overcame the Roman Empire because the early Christians "outlived, outdied, and outthought" their contemporaries. "You will know them by their fruits," Jesus had said, and he left his followers with only one commandment: "That you love one another as I have loved you." There is no other way in which the Church can minister the grace of God. Not by the size of its memberships, not by the correctness of its doctrine, not by the splendor of its architecture nor by the beauty of its liturgy will Christ measure his Church. His measure will be the quality of its life. The communion of saints must express the communion of the Holy Spirit. Luke says that the Church grew because its members were having favor with all the people. In this, after all, the Church was but reflecting the life of Him who himself "increased in wisdom and in stature, and in favor with God and man."

> "Follow with reverent steps the great example
> Of Him whose holy work was doing good;
> So shall the wide earth seem our Father's temple,
> Each loving life a psalm of gratitude."

One of our Communion prayers expresses it: "So enrich us by Thy continual grace that the life of Jesus may be made manifest in our mortal body, and Thy kingdom be furthered through all such good works as Thou hast prepared for us to walk in."

Luke concludes: "And the Lord added to their number day by day those who were being saved." We witness this growth as we witness the reception of new members to the Lord's Table. The Communion translates The Acts of the Apostles into The Acts of Today, as the living Christ links us in glad and grateful communion with all who are his family.

15

COMMUNION AND COMMITMENT

*The cup of blessing which we bless, is it not the communion
of the blood of Christ? The bread which we break, is it not the
communion of the body of Christ? . . . We being many are
one bread, and one body: for we are all partakers of that one
bread.*

I Cor. 10:16, 17 (K.J.V.)

WHAT is the Church? The Apostles' Creed confesses the
reality of " the holy Catholic Church, the communion
of saints." With a wealth of imagery, the New Testament pictures the Church as the bride of Christ, as the flock of the
Good Shepherd, as the building built upon the foundation of
Christ, as the branches of the Vine. Paul's favorite figure, however, is that of the body. The Church is the body of Christ. It
is in Christ that " the whole body, joined and knit together by
every joint with which it is supplied, when each part is working
properly, makes bodily growth and upbuilds itself in love."
" Now you are the body of Christ and individually members of
it." For Paul this unity of the body is best expressed in the
Lord's Supper: " The cup of blessing which we bless, is it not
the communion of the blood of Christ? The bread which we
break, is it not the communion of the body of Christ? . . . We
being many are one bread, and one body: for we are all partakers of that one bread " (K.J.V.).

It is a noble conception, but is it not a tantalizing dream?

Can we speak of one "holy Catholic Church" — when Christendom is divided into conflicting churches? Can we speak of the body of Christ — when even an individual congregation witnesses to division and strife? To be sure, nowadays Christians are trying as never before to witness to unity in a divided world. We are no longer content with our divisions when we listen with new earnestness to our Lord's prayer " that they may all be one." Nonetheless, the unity of the Church is still obscured in the rival claims of the churches, and the "communion of saints" is still hindered when Christians can neither agree nor sit down with one another at the Communion Table. It is a lovely vision — but is Paul not dreaming? Or was the Church he knew different from the Church we know today?

Was Paul writing to the Church of his dreams? Hardly. Let him speak: " When you assemble as a church, I hear that there are divisions among you; and I partly believe it, for there must be factions among you." That does not sound like a dream. Indeed, Paul devotes these pages to his picture of the Church as the body of Christ precisely because men were forgetting it. The Corinthian Church had some of the same ailments of " preacher partisans " and snobbishness that beset us still. It is in the context of church disorder that Paul is writing. Even the Lord's Supper, he complains, has become a source of division. " Part of the dark background of the passage," comments John Short in *The Interpreter's Bible*, " is the disorder in the church meeting at Corinth; part of it is the apostle's breaking heart as he braces himself for the application of aseptic and astringent words with a view to healing the grievous hurt done to the Christian fellowship." Might Paul not be writing today?

And yet, for Paul the unity of the body of Christ remains. The question is not whether there is a " holy Catholic Church," the question is only whether we share in its life. This awareness undergirds all of Paul's effort, and it gives him the confidence that the congregation at Corinth too may share in the life of the beloved community.

This does not imply that we may gloss over the sins of disorder. On the contrary, for Paul such manifestations of selfishness are nothing less than demonic, and, he adds, " You cannot drink the cup of the Lord and the cup of demons." There is a solemn choice, for no man can serve two masters. But, he would say, we do not need to choose the table of demons for we have the Table of the Lord. The communion of saints, the beloved community, is not something we build or manipulate with clever stratagems. It is here — if we will but share it and live it. " The cup of blessing which we bless, is it not a participation in the blood of Christ? The bread which we break, is it not a participation in the body of Christ? " (R.S.V.).

This communion exists through the body and blood of Christ. Christian fellowship rests, not upon airy ideals, but upon the historical reality of the Word made flesh. We do not reach up for this life; this life has come down to our life. Our only abiding communion draws its reality from Him who has come to take our death that he might give us his life. That is why the Lord's Supper is forever dear to Christian faith — it takes us to the very heart of faith. " There is one God, and there is one mediator between God and man, the man Christ Jesus." Together, we draw in memory " beneath the cross of Jesus."

The body and the blood of Christ, however, suggest something beyond the memory of Calvary. At the cross, says *Piers Plowman*, " blood brothers we became there and gentlemen each one." We are blood brothers because we participate now in the life or " blood " of Jesus Christ. Paul is not only thinking of the blood shed in sacrificial love at Calvary; he is also expressing here the reality of a new life in Christ. The Supper is communion as well as memory. The living Christ is here to give us his life.

> " One Bread, one Cup, one Body, we,
>   United by our life in Thee."

Paul would add one thing. Our communion must become commitment. We call the Supper our " sacrament," which in early usage meant the oath that soldiers took to swear they would not desert their posts but would follow their emperor in arduous campaigns. In similar fashion, our sacrament is not an escape from a divided and distracted world. If we, "though many, are one body" as recipients of Christ's life, then we being many must also become one in outward experience and service. The Lord's Supper forbids us to be content with any *status quo* in world or Church.

According to medieval legend, before King Arthur sent his knights on errantry to right wrongs and befriend the helpless, he would call them together at his round table, where each knight could see the face of his king and the faces of his fellows. Shall the followers of the King of Kings do less?

> "And when we leave Thy table, Lord,
>   And go into the world again,
>   Help us to carry with us there
>   The savour of that holy fare,
>   And prove the virtue of The Word
>   To other men."

16

THE SUPPER OF THE LAMB

Then I heard what seemed to be the voice of a great multitude,
like the sound of many waters and like the sound of mighty
thunderpeals, crying,
   " Hallelujah! For the Lord our God the Almighty reigns.
   Let us rejoice and exult and give him the glory,
   for the marriage of the Lamb has come,
   and his Bride has made herself ready;
   it was granted her to be clothed with fine linen, bright and
      pure " —
for the fine linen is the righteous deeds of the saints.
   And the angel said to me, "Write this: Blessed are those
who are invited to the marriage supper of the Lamb."

Rev. 19:6–9

THE author of this strangely magnificent book was able to
live life on two levels. Over one environment he had no
control. " I . . . was on the island called Patmos." Imprisoned
for his faith, he shares fully the grim reality of a world of
tragedy and evil. He has, however, another environment which
no temporal circumstances can destroy. " I was in the Spirit
on the Lord's day." Because he lived in the dimension of
eternity as well as of time, John could see beyond the limits of
the temporal to the goal of all time and to the very meaning
of existence. At the heart of the universe he sees a throne. And
before the throne he sees a Lamb, while through the corridors

of heaven he hears the chorus of the redeemed. " I heard what seemed to be the voice of a great multitude, like the sound of many waters and like the sound of mighty thunderpeals, crying,

" ' Hallelujah! For the Lord our God the Almighty reigns.
Let us rejoice and exult and give him the glory,
for the marriage of the Lamb has come.' "

Out of earth's separations he sees the fellowship of eternity. Beyond the travail of history he sees the triumph of God. " For thine is the kingdom and the power and the glory, forever! "

Such a vision is not conjured up to satisfy some idle curiosity or to provide a dream-world escape. The man who caught this vision was able to live triumphantly today because he was sure of tomorrow. You and I stand where he stood — in a world of tragedy and haunting fear. But, if we are Christians, do we not also stand with him in the dimension of eternity? Can you not also say, " I was in the Spirit on the Lord's day? " Does not the universe have a throne? Then, *sursum corda* — lift up your hearts! The Lord God Omnipotent reigns.

What makes John's vision relevant to his time and ours is the figure of Him who stands before the throne. John saw " a Lamb standing, as though it had been slain," and it is this Lamb who holds the clue to the drama of history. The Lord of eternity the Lamb that was slain! John knows this Lamb. He knows him as " Jesus Christ the faithful witness, the first-born of the dead, and the ruler of kings on earth." Heaven is not remote from earth's sorrows, nor is heaven's throne occupied by a distant deity. " To him who loves us and has freed us from our sins by his blood and made us a kingdom, priests to his God and Father, to him be glory and dominion for ever and ever. Amen. Behold, he is coming with the clouds, and every eye will see him, every one who has pierced him." Sovereignty and sacrifice, power and pardon, lordship and lowliness have met forever in the heart of eternity, to bring heaven and earth together.

Can we catch something of that magnificent certainty? Can

we see Jesus Christ the same yesterday, today, and forever? Can we see beyond the temporal to the eternal love of God? " As it is," says the New Testament, " we do not yet see everything in subjection to him. But we see Jesus." We see Jesus!

> " Peace, perfect peace, our future all unknown?
> Jesus we know, and He is on the throne."

John sees not only the throne and the Lamb. He sees also a great multitude that no man can number, from every nation and tribe and tongue, standing before the throne. Again and again he hears the voice of this multitude as the chorus of the redeemed swells from crescendo to crescendo in exulting praise. Now the full wonder of salvation and communion is pictured as a nuptial feast. " Blessed are those who are invited to the marriage supper of the Lamb."

> " O blest communion, fellowship divine!
> We feebly struggle, they in glory shine;
> Yet all are one in Thee, for all are Thine.
> Alleluia! Alleluia! "

Is the vision far away and unattainable? Then let God speak to us now in tangible sign and symbol. The Supper of the Lamb is already given in this Supper of the Lord. " For as often as you eat this bread and drink the cup, you proclaim the Lord's death until he comes."

" Blessed are those who are invited." Our love does not have to bend the love of God toward us. Were that so, we should forever be condemned by the knowledge of our failures and limitations. Can the sinful approach the Holy or the temporal climb to the Eternal? For who can endure the day of his coming, and who can stand when he appears? But be of good cheer. Here and hereafter the Supper declares faith's deepest certainty. God invites us to fellowship. We are those who are invited. The whole story of salvation is the story of God's persistent invitation to fellowship. " Come now, let us reason together, says the Lord; though your sins are like scarlet, they shall be white

as snow; though they are red like crimson, they shall become
like wool." " Come to me, all who labor and are heavy-laden,
and I will give you rest." " Come, O blessed of my Father, in-
herit the kingdom prepared for you from the foundation of the
world." " The Spirit and the Bride say, ' Come.' And let him
who hears say, ' Come.' And let him who is thirsty come, let
him who desires take the water of life without price." If Christianity were one more impossible ethic, its great word would
be " do." Because Christianity is first of all a gospel, its great
word is " come." " O Lamb of God, I come."

I come — but I do not come alone. In his temporal environment John is painfully aware of loneliness and separation, for
he is but one of the scattered children of God. Now, as he sees
the throne and the Lamb, he sees himself surrounded by a
multitude that no man can number. From every nation and
tongue he sees the redeemed family of God united at the
Supper of the Lamb. He knows that the Church is more than
an association of scattered individuals — it is the bride of Christ

> " Yet she on earth hath union
> With God the Three in One,
> And mystic sweet communion
> With those whose rest is won."

Christendom may still have its unhappy divisions, earth may
still have its painful separations, but John knows that God's
purpose is not complete until all the ransomed hosts are one in
the banquet hall of God. He knows that the " communion of
saints " is a blessed reality, and that Jesus' prayer is being fulfilled, " that they may all be one."

> " With our sainted ones in glory
> Seated at our Father's board,
> May the Church that waiteth for Thee
> Keep love's tie unbroken, Lord."

" Then I heard what seemed to be the voice of a great multitude, like the sound of many waters and like the sound of

mighty thunderpeals, crying 'Hallelujah!' " Yes, blessed are
those who are invited to the Supper of the Lamb.

But, you say, John is still on Patmos, and we are still en-
meshed in the burdens of the present. Aye, but John is " in the
Spirit." He may not know what tomorrow will bring, but he
knows who holds tomorrow. His vision is no fantasy, for its
promise is already actualized in the present. The Supper of the
Lamb is already seen and sealed in the Supper of the crucified
and risen Christ. It is " the guarantee of our inheritance until
we acquire possession of it, to the praise of his glory."

" And the angel said to me, ' Write this: Blessed are those
who are invited to the marriage supper of the Lamb.' " Every
voice of Christian experience says to us, " Blessed are those
who are invited to the Supper of the Lamb." " Blessed are those
who hunger and thirst for righteousness, for they shall be satisfied."

SELF–EXAMINATION

17

"SOMETIMES IT CAUSES ME
TO TREMBLE"

As they were eating, he said, "Truly, I say to you, one of you will betray me." And they were very sorrowful, and began to say to him one after another, "Is it I, Lord?"

MATT. 26:21

Let a man examine himself, and so eat of the bread and drink of the cup. For any one who eats and drinks without discerning the body eats and drinks judgment upon himself.

I COR. 11:28

THAT the Lord's Supper is a judgment comes as a jarring and disquieting realization to disciples. They know that Jesus has his enemies without, but it is upsetting to discover that he may have enemies within. "Truly, . . . one of you will betray me." His word staggers them. "They were very sorrowful, and began to say to him one after another, 'Is it I, Lord?'" The scene may pivot around Judas, but is certainly not confined to Judas. Suddenly not one of them feels safe, and anxiety grips each heart: "Is it I, Lord?"

An old spiritual asks, "Were you there when they crucified my Lord?" and answers, "Sometimes it causes me to tremble." Perhaps this question of the Supper ought to make us tremble. "Let a man examine himself," says Paul, "and so eat of the bread and drink of the cup. For any one who eats and drinks without discerning the body eats and drinks judgment upon himself."

"Is it I, Lord?" Three facts of Christian experience are implied in the anxious question.

For one thing, it reveals *how little I know myself*. It may be that the disciples ask the question in part to justify themselves — "Surely, it could not be I!" But the defense soon breaks down into deeper anxiety. Not a man is sure of himself. The scene epitomizes what modern psychology is realizing increasingly — the unconscious, hidden self that lies within each of us.

Take Peter, for example. He seems so sure of himself, pledging that he is ready to follow Jesus to prison and to death. The prophecy of denial seems utterly incredible to him.

> "Ashamed of Jesus! sooner far
> Let evening blush to own a star."

Ah, don't be so sure, Peter! You too are in danger. It is easy to point a finger at Judas, but once the dark design now forming in his mind seemed as incredible to him as the thought of denial seems to you. And, for a moment, Peter seems to realize it — "Is it I, Lord?"

How little we know ourselves! The Old Testament tells a vivid story of the prophet Elisha going to Damascus to confront the king's courtier, Hazael. Elisha stared at the courtier until he felt ashamed, and then he burst into tears. When asked why, the prophet replied, "Because I know the evil that you will do." And he proceeds to unfold a tale of violence and treachery so appalling that the horrified Hazael cries out, "Am I a dog that I should do this?" Yet soon, all too soon, the incredible became bloody fact. Again and again, life has underscored the apostle's warning, "Therefore let any one who thinks that he stands take heed lest he fall."

Come back to Peter. In John's account, Jesus rises from table and begins to wash the disciples' feet, saying, "You are clean, but not all of you." In her play *The King's Supper*, Dorothy Sayers has Peter whisper to John, "John, why does he say that we are not all clean?" And John whispers back, "I don't know,

Peter, but when I look into my heart, I find it full of unswept,
dusty corners." Is any one of us safe? We begin to see the force
of Jesus' prayer: " Lead us not into temptation, but deliver us
from evil." " Is it I, Lord? "

> " Each one looked inward, frightened lest he find
>   A shoddy place where he had dreamed of steel.
> None placed the guilt on any other guest
>   Who had partaken of that gracious meal."
>   — *Helen Welshimer*.

Again, the question reveals *how little I know my Lord*. That
is our deeper problem. These men love their Master, but they
understand him so little. They want him to fit their plans, and
they have not learned to surrender their plans for his. Even in
the sanctity of this upper room, their failure to understand is
painfully apparent. Even at the table, they quarrel as to who
will be greatest. Even when Jesus has washed their feet, he must
ask, " Do you know what I have done to you? " All through
that evening their questions continue to reveal how little they
know him. " Lord, we do not know where you are going; how
can we know the way? " " Lord, show us the Father, and we
shall be satisfied." Jesus' reply is full of pathos: " Have I been
with you so long, and yet do you not know me? "

Twenty centuries have passed, and still Jesus says, " Have I
been with you so long, and yet do you not know me? " Is this not
disquieting? If to the men who had journeyed and fellowshiped
with him he was still a stranger, is it not more disquieting that
centuries later he still is a stranger to those who follow him?
Dostoevsky's Grand Inquisitor is the perfect parable of how this
can happen when a man or a church sets out to correct Christ's
work for him. " We have corrected thy work," says the proud
ecclesiastic. " Why hast thou come now to hinder us? And why
dost thou look silently and searchingly at me with thy mild
eyes? " " Truly, I say to you, one of you will betray me." This
is the judgment of the Lord's Supper. " Any one who eats and
drinks without discerning the body eats and drinks judgment
upon himself."

Happily, there is something more to be said. The question
also reveals *how deeply my Lord knows me, and how deeply he
loves.* Look at the scene once more. "The Lord Jesus on the
night when he was betrayed took bread." W. M. Clow, with
fine insight, suggests that the apostle here is not only marking
a point in time; he is pointing a contrast between sin and grace,
between our treachery and Christ's faithfulness. Think of it!
On the night when he was betrayed, Jesus took bread and gave
it, saying, "This is my body which is broken for you."

How well he knows them! "Simon, Simon," he says to Peter,
"Satan demanded to have you . . . but I have prayed for you."
And Judas? Jesus knows — and Judas knows that he knows —
and still Jesus washes his feet and touches his hand at table,
and even yet would welcome him back. If only Judas had stayed!
But he does not want to meet the eyes of the Master, and he
rushes out into the night.

How well he knows us! He welcomes us to his Table of fellowship and forgiveness. This is what turns the judgment of
the Supper into salvation. It is precisely because he knows me
so well that he comes to me. It is because he loves me so deeply
that he takes my sin.

"Is it I, Lord?" Yes, indeed. I find myself as I find my Lord.
The psalmist's confession is mine as I come to the Supper:

> "O Lord, thou hast searched me and known me!
>   Thou knowest when I sit down and when I rise up;
>
> .   .   .   .
>
> Thou searchest out my path and my lying down,
>   and art acquainted with all my ways."

But faith welcomes this examination rather than flees from it,
for the Searcher of hearts is the Saviour of men:

> "Search me, O God, and know my heart!
>   Try me, and know my thoughts!
> And see if there be any wicked way in me,
>   and lead me in the way everlasting!"

18

"THE OUTSIDE OF THE CUP"

Then you will begin to say, "We ate and drank in your presence, and you taught in our streets." But he will say, "I tell you, I do not know where you come from."

LUKE 13:26

And the Lord said to him, "Now you Pharisees cleanse the outside of the cup."

LUKE 11:37

WORSHIP is not necessarily a good thing, for worship can be our judgment as well as our salvation. It is one thing to be interested in worship; it is quite another thing to worship God. This is true even of our celebration of the Lord's Supper.

Perhaps this is why Jesus refused to deal with religious curiosity, and dealt only with religious concern. When a Samaritan woman tried to evade the moral implications of worship by becoming "interested in" religious places and methods, Jesus brushed aside her questions by saying, "Neither on this mountain nor in Jerusalem." He did not mean that worship is unimportant; he did mean that worship is useless unless it is "in spirit and truth." It was only when the Samaritan woman had passed from religious curiosity to ultimate concern that her worship became discovery of Christ.

Again, when someone asked him, "Lord, will those who are saved be few?" Jesus did not answer the curiosity. He made it, instead, a matter of personal concern: "Strive to enter by the narrow door; for many, I tell you, will seek to enter and will not be able." It will be, he continued, as when a householder shuts the door and many who had taken him for granted suddenly find themselves excluded, and begin to knock and plead, "We ate and drank in your presence." To them the master must reply, "I do not know . . . you." "Not every one who says . . . , 'Lord, Lord,' shall enter the kingdom of heaven." The trouble with you devotees of worship, said Jesus to a Pharisee, is that you cleanse only the outside of the cup.

These are sobering words. Suppose they were Christ's judgment upon our sacramental observance? Suppose we are those who say, "We ate and drank in your presence"? Suppose Jesus were saying to us that we got no farther than the outside of the cup? "Let a man examine himself, and so eat of the bread and drink of the cup." Let us be honest. What does our worship, especially our sacramental worship, mean to us?

There are many ways in which worship can remain "the outside of the cup." One of the most deadening things that can happen to religion is formalism. Whenever ritual becomes an end in itself, the life has gone out of it, and we touch only the outside of the cup.

> "In vain we tune our formal songs,
> In vain we strive to rise;
> Hosannas languish on our tongues,
> And our devotion dies."

Again, religious worship reaches only the outside of the cup if it does not pass beyond aesthetic enjoyment. This is a subtle temptation. Certainly we must worship God in the beauty of holiness. We do God no honor by making our worship drab and dull. It is a pity that some forms of Protestant reaction to Roman sacramentalism took the form of iconoclasm in Church architecture, ritual, and music. We can be grateful that today we are returning to a deeper sense of worship and to a greater appreciation of a reverent liturgy. Yet always there is the danger that we might measure the quality of our worship by aesthetic enjoyment rather than by a genuine encounter with the living God. If we only " enjoy the service," if we have been moved more by the atmosphere of worship than by the Word and will of God, have we truly met with God? Of no part of our worship is this more true than of our observance of the Lord's Supper. It is a pathetic irony that our expression " hocus-pocus " has been assumed to derive from the words of the Table, " *Hoc est corpus* " (this is the body), illustrating how liturgy can become remote from communion with God. Kierkegaard was not wrong when he suggested that we must pass beyond the levels of aesthetic and moral experience to the level of religious experience.

Notice that he insists we must pass beyond the moral, as well as beyond the aesthetic. It was to a moralist that Jesus made the remark concerning the outside of the cup. The spirit of moralism can be the death knell of religion, for it is apt to make of religion a set of rules instead of a gracious communion. A religion of works brings no peace with God, as Paul discovered. If the ego needs purifying, then all the outward activities are still unavailing, no matter how earnest the effort. " Wretched man that I am! " cried Paul, " Who will deliver me? "

> " Not the labors of my hands
>   Can fulfill Thy law's demands;
>   Could my zeal no respite know,
>   Could my tears forever flow,
>   All for sin could not atone;
>   Thou must save, and Thou alone."

The outside of the cup! Whenever worship is empty form, or artistic enjoyment, or moralistic endeavor, it is still the worship of self and not communion with God. Even the Table of the Lord can become a sorry pretense and a futile pleading that " we ate and drank in your presence." Even the cup of communion can remain only the outside of the cup.

Why should we be content with the outside of the cup,

when Christ offers us the inside of the cup? " This is my blood
of the covenant, which is poured out for many." God has something better for us than the outside of the cup. " The hour is
coming, and now is, when the true worshipers will worship
the Father in spirit and truth, for such the Father seeks to
worship him." And the Father is known in the Son. His presence is the inside of the cup.

That is to say, when we fasten our attention in Communion
only upon the elements of bread and wine, or argue as to the
relative merits of open or close Communion, or discuss the
proper frequency of observance — we are looking at the outside
of the cup and not yet communing with Christ. It is not that
these are unimportant matters; manifestly, they must be con-
sidered. But they have meaning only in the measure to which
they draw us to Christ himself. Similarly, our desire for the
proper atmosphere of worship, with a proper blending of word
and hymnody, is relevant only so far as it leads us to him. Above
all, the presence of Christ will mean the end of a religion of
moralistic pretension. " For no human being will be justified
in his sight by works of the law since through the law comes
knowledge of sin. . . . By grace you have been saved through
faith, and this is not your own doing, it is the gift of God." It
is just at this point, one suspects, that so many sincerely religious people miss the way. They have not yet learned to let
go of the self's pretensions of goodness, and have not yet
truly clasped in faith that nail-scarred hand of the Son of God.
Faith, after all, means to let go of self in order to cling to the
love that will not let us go.

Well, what does this Communion bring us? The outside of
the cup — or the inside? When we come away from this Table,
what has happened? Shall we be able only to say, " We ate and
drank in your presence," without actually touching that presence? Or will Jesus' promise be fulfilled in us, that " he who
eats my flesh and drinks my blood has eternal life "? Why
should we be satisfied with anything less than the inside of the
cup — the life he wants so much to give us? " ' Why do you

spend your money for that which is not bread, and your labor for that which does not satisfy? . . . Seek the Lord while he may be found, call upon him while he is near.' " And can he be nearer than in this sacrament of his love?

> " Thou, O Christ, art all I want;
> More than all in Thee I find."

19

MY WAYS ARE NOT YOUR WAYS

John the Baptist has come eating no bread and drinking no wine; and you say, "He has a demon." The Son of man has come eating and drinking; and you say, "Behold a glutton and a drunkard, a friend of tax collectors and sinners!" Yet wisdom is justified by all her children.

LUKE 7:33-35

RELIGION is the way a man faces life. Since there are different ways of facing life, there are different religious approaches. One is self-denial; another is self-expression. One makes of life a fast; another makes it a feast. One lives as a stranger in the world of time and sense; another is so much at home here that he is stranger to the world of eternity.

The Word of God points us beyond all our ways. "My thoughts are not your thoughts, neither are your ways my ways, says the Lord." The pity is, we are so often absorbed in our own ways that we do not recognize the way of God who is in our midst. We are, says Jesus, like children who are play-acting at life. "To what . . . shall I compare the men of this generation . . . ? They are like children sitting in the market place and calling . . . ,

'We piped to you, and you did not dance;
We wailed, and you did not weep.'

For John the Baptist has come eating no bread and drinking no wine; and you say, 'He has a demon.' The Son of man has come eating and drinking; and you say, ' Behold a glutton and a drunkard, a friend of tax collectors and sinners! ' Yet wisdom is justified by all her children."

Jesus' words apply to our generation. We still are like children play-acting at life, so engrossed in our own ways of facing life that we busily make everything an either-or of our own choosing, while we fail to recognize the God who is in our midst, whose ways are not our ways and whose thoughts are not our thoughts.

On the one hand, the ascetic too easily denies that the earth is the Lord's and the fullness thereof. He is all too prone to make of religion a " touch not; taste not; handle not " (K.J.V.). Is it not denying God the Creator to scorn his world of time and sense? Is it not a distortion of Christianity to make life here of no importance, to act as though the body were the prison of the soul, and to damn history as a hopeless fatality rather than to acknowledge it as the arena of God's loving purpose? Such " spirituality " is not the religion of Jesus who came as a friend of the home, who rejoiced in his Father's world, who fed the hungry and healed the sick, and who taught us to pray, " Give us this day our daily bread."

However, if such world rejection is not the way of the Son of Man, neither is the religion of self-expression. Our generation is more inclined to self-assertion than it is tempted to a morbid self-rejection. Many live by the creed of " eat, drink, be merry." We pride ourselves on trying to live in " one world at a time," forgetting that we are meant to be citizens of two worlds, the temporal and the eternal. " Our commonwealth is in heaven," says Paul, and we are false to our heritage if we are ready to sell our full birthright for a sorry mess of pottage. If this is our Father's world, it is also true that the world can be " too much with us." Jesus, who taught us to pray for daily bread, knew that man cannot live by bread alone. He who fed the body also urged men not to labor for the food which perishes. He who repudiated a religion of mere negation, and who answered his critics by suggesting that people do not fast while the Bridegroom is with them, also knew that prayer and fasting can discipline the spirit and overcome the evil one. Jesus is not John the Baptist, for he comes with the wine of God's love as well as with the water of repentance. Yet Jesus is glad to hail John as the greatest of those born of women.

His ways are not our ways. We see the way of the Son of Man best in the Supper. Our partial truths too easily obscure the way of the Lord of life. " John the Baptist has come eating no bread and drinking no wine; and you say, ' He has a demon.' The Son of man has come eating and drinking; and you say, ' Behold a glutton and a drunkard, a friend of tax collectors and sinners! ' Yet wisdom is justified by all her children."

Let us be glad that the Son of Man has come eating and drinking. Nowhere is the way and will of Christ more clearly seen than in his Table. Bread and wine belong to the physical world, and a purely otherworldly religion would scorn such material emblems as unworthy channels of the presence of God. But Jesus, who knew God as the good Creator of matter and of spirit, does not scorn God's world. He knew that we are creatures of flesh and spirit, and he knew that the whole man can be addressed by God. " Handle me, and see," says the risen Lord to his disciples. " Handle me, and see . . . that it is I myself." " O taste and see that the Lord is good! " The body is not the prison of the soul; rather is it the temple of the spirit. The gospel is good news precisely because it declares that " the Word became flesh " — and the Word becomes flesh anew in the bread and wine of Communion. This is our answer to those who mistake Christianity for some misty idealism remote from real life. So Paul, at least, answered his " spiritual " critics. " This is my defense to those who would examine me. Do we not have the right to our food and drink? " Yes, the Son of Man has come eating and drinking. Let us thank God that he did.

And yet the Word, while it becomes flesh, is ever more than flesh, and the presence of Christ can never be confined or contained in these elements of bread and wine. The material is not

an end in itself — it is sacramental, the instrument and chan-
nel of the spirit. Lest men forget this, Paul warned the church
of Corinth not to let the Supper become an occasion for in-
temperance. " When you meet together, it is not the Lord's
supper that you eat. For in eating, each one goes ahead with
his own meal, and one is hungry and another is drunk." Our
Lord also insisted that " it is the spirit that gives life, the flesh
is of no avail; the words that I have spoken to you are spirit
and life."

" My ways are not your ways," says the Lord. Neither in
fasting nor in feasting, but in finding Christ, lies the secret of
Communion.

And we can find him, for he has found us. The Son of Man
has come eating and drinking, and men called him the friend
of sinners. The word of scorn becomes the badge of love and
the assurance of faith. A friend of sinners — that is what I need,
for

> " I am both weak and sinful,
>   But this I surely know,
> The Lord came down to save me
>   Because He loved me so."

It comes to this. Not in our ways, but in his way, lies our
salvation. As Augustine put it long ago: " Walk by him the
man and thou comest to God. By him thou goest, to him thou
goest. Look not for any way except himself by which to come
to him. For if he had not vouchsafed to be the way we should
all have gone astray. Therefore he became the way by which
thou shouldst come. I do not say to thee, seek the way. The
way itself is come to thee: arise and walk."

Jesus said after the supper, " Arise, let us go hence."

20

"FOOD FOR THE FED UP"

*"Why do you spend your money for
that which is not bread,
and your labor for that which
does not satisfy?"*

ISA. 55:2

"I am the bread of life."
JOHN 6:48

THE prophet's question is well put. Why do we spend our lives for that which does not satisfy? Studdert-Kennedy, one of the gallant spirits of our century, asks the same question in a book called *Food for the Fed Up*. One of the most expressive phrases in our vocabulary, he holds, are the words, " I'm fed up." They express all the waste and futility, the boredom of activity without purpose, the tragedy of life crammed but unsatisfied. " It is like trying to live on fancy cakes — little bits of God knows what with cherries on top — pure sensations without satisfaction. You cannot live on them. You must have bread and butter, solid food; if you try a diet of fancy cakes you get fed up, which means that you are hungry still, but can't eat."

It often happens. Multitudes of people live only for pleasure. Their creed is, " Eat, drink, be merry." The trouble, of course, is that such merriment doesn't last. The writer of Ecclesiastes learned this lesson from bitter experience: " I said to myself, ' Come now, I will make a test of pleasure; enjoy yourself.' But behold, this also was vanity. I said of laughter, 'It is mad,' and of pleasure, 'What use is it?' . . . Behold all was vanity and a striving after wind." Why do we labor for that which is not bread?

> "I have had my will,
>   Tasted every pleasure,
> I have drunk my fill
>   Of the purple measure,
> Life has lost its zest,
> Sorrow is my guest.
>   O, the lees are bitter, bitter!
> Give me rest."
> — *George Arnold.*

There is no more pathetic sight than a man vainly trying to cram his fed up life with pleasures that do not feed the aching hunger of his soul. Housman put it in expressive language:

> "Could men be drunk forever
>   With liquor, love, or fights,
> Lief would I rise at morning
>   And lief lie down by nights.
> But men at times are sober
>   And think by fits and starts,
> And when they think they fasten
>   Their hands upon their hearts."

Others try to cram their lives with possessions, only to discover that "a man's life does not consist in the abundance of his possessions." Anyway, "you can't take it with you." Jesus aptly described the futility of such acquisition in his parable of the foolish rich man who spent his whole life trying to possess, only to hear God's judgment say at the last: "Fool! This night your soul is required of you; and the things you have prepared, whose will they be? "

Why do you spend your money for that which is not bread, and your labor for that which does not satisfy? Why look for

further illustrations — the truth of the prophetic protest is plain
enough. We cram our lives only to be fed up — and hungry still.

What is it that we need and want most? What do we really
hunger for? Browning knew:

> " O God, where do they tend, these struggling aims?
>   What would I have? What is the ' sleep ' which seems
>   To bound all? Can there be a ' waking ' point
>   Of crowning life? . . .
>   The last point I can trace is — rest beneath
>   Some better essence than itself, in weakness;
>   This is ' myself,' not what I think should be:
>   And what is that I hunger for but God? "

When all is said, we are hungry for God, and nothing else will
do. " Peace with God," writes Studdert-Kennedy again, " is the
one absolute necessity of the fully human life: it is the plain
bread which every soul must have in order to live. He may not
be always conscious of his need. Bread is what every man needs,
and no man thinks of wanting until he has to go without it."
Wisdom, then, lies in recognizing our hunger. " Blessed are
those who hunger and thirst for righteousness, for they shall be
satisfied."

But can this hunger be filled? What if God and his righteousness were inaccessible to us? What if the peace and certainty
for which we crave must forever elude us? Here the Supper of
the Lord can speak. " I am the bread of life," says Jesus. " I am
the living bread which came down from heaven; if any one eats
of this bread he will live for ever; and the bread which I shall
give for the life of the world is my flesh." These words, actualized in the Supper, are the good news of God — " Jesus Christ
and him crucified."

Jesus Christ. Christian faith centers not in principles but in
a person. Man's hunger for God can be satisfied with nothing
less than God himself in personal, loving relationship. Can we
by searching find out God? Is it not rather that God has come
to us? " The Word became flesh and dwelt among us . . . ;

we have beheld his glory." Jesus does more than bring us God's
Word — he *is* God's Word. Jesus does more than witness to the
Father — " I and the Father are one." Jesus does more than
diagnose our deepest hunger — he meets that hunger as he says,
" I am the bread of life." The living God is not unknowable
majesty but reconciling love. " God was in Christ reconciling
the world to himself."

The Supper leads us on: Jesus Christ — and him crucified.
" The bread which I shall give for the life of the world is my
flesh." " This is my body . . . broken for you." Christ, as the
perfect revelation of the righteousness of God, would still be
an impossible ideal unless Christ crucified had brought that
righteousness into our lives. Christ crucified means that in very
deed the Word has been made flesh and blood in utter self-
sacrifice. Christ crucified means that he truly gives himself.
" For my flesh is food indeed, and my blood is drink indeed."

We must have God. Why should we try to fill our lives with
futile and fevered striving, when all the while God is waiting to
give us the bread for which we hunger? " It is your Father's
good pleasure to give you the kingdom." He gives it here — in
the Supper of his love.

> " From the best bliss that earth imparts
> We turn unfilled to Thee again.
>
> .   .   .   .
>
> " We taste Thee, O Thou living Bread,
> And long to feast upon Thee still.
> We drink of Thee, the Fountainhead,
> And thirst our souls from Thee to fill."

21

THE ULTIMATE QUESTION

When they had finished breakfast, Jesus said to Simon Peter, "Simon, son of John, do you love me?"

JOHN 21:15

Tʜɪs epilogue from John's Gospel really says all there is to say. It throws a flood of light upon our time and upon our lives. We live in a time full of questions. Inevitably we bring some of these questions with us when we worship. How does Christ come to us? What does he expect of us? Where will he take us?

In the days that followed the resurrection, the disciples of Jesus had many questions. They did not know what tomorrow would bring. They wondered if it might be like yesterday's experience of Christ, but they soon learned that resurrection is not resuscitation, that the Christian road leads on, not back. Yet where? Uncertainty made them restless, and Peter said: "I'm going fishing. I've got to do something." "We'll go with you," they said, and so they tried to find satisfaction in the old life — but they caught nothing. Then, says the Gospel, as the dawn was breaking after a night of uncertainty, Jesus Christ appeared to them. Even then they did not immediately recognize him until they heard his familiar voice as he took bread and gave it to them.

It is an intimate picture, for it focuses quickly upon two persons — Peter and his Lord. Communion with Christ is always a deeply personal experience, as we meet our Lord. Who is Peter? You are that man — and I. Peter sums up all the lights and shadows of our experience: one moment a rock of faith, the next moment unstable as water. Peter has had a bad time of it lately, for he is haunted by painful memories of denial. However, in this repast with the risen Lord, Peter discovers that Christ has come to restore him to discipleship. Three times Peter had denied. Three times now he may pledge his love.

Peter has many questions to ask his Lord. Who has not? All the disciples had questions enough: "Lord, when shall these things be?" "Lord, will you at this time restore the kingdom to Israel?" "Lord, show us the way." Apparently, disciples are often quite as baffled by life's questions as any others. The difference, perhaps, is that disciples can bring their questions to Christ. Yet it is worth noticing that they do not always receive the answers they think they need. When they ask, "When will this be?" all that Jesus replies is: "It is not for you to know times or seasons. Watch and pray." When they ask, "Lord, show us the way," all he replies is, "I am the way."

This is not to suggest that faith should stifle its questions. It would be a shallow faith that had no questions, and where shall we bring our questions if not to Christ? Surely, he who himself cried out, "My God, my God, why?" — surely he understands our questions. Disciples need not be ashamed of questions.

And yet disciples need something more than answers to their questions. Peter soon discovers that Christ has not met him here to satisfy his curiosity about the future. Instead, Peter finds that Christ has met him here to ask him a question of his own.

That question is primary and fundamental: "Simon, son of John, do you love me?" Peter had failed in Jerusalem, not because he had not had enough answers for his questions. Peter had failed because he had not adequately answered the question of his Lord.

"Simon, son of John, do you love me?" How shall we answer that question? We are apt to come to Communion with many questions of our own, but let us not crowd out the question of our Lord. It is not always easy to answer his question. It can be a shattering but a saving experience. Once Peter would have answered glibly and confidently: "Of course, Lord. I'll go where you want me to go. Though all others forsake you, I'll never desert you." But not now. A chastened Peter is mindful of his failure. Indeed, Peter does not even dare to use the word "love" which Jesus uses. That word (*agape*) in the New Testament is drawn out of obscurity to become the most expressive word for the kind of love that God has for us — utterly self-giving, self-forgetting love. "Simon, son of John, do you love me?" Peter replies, "Lord, you know that I'm your friend — you know that I mean to be yours." Jesus accepts the intent of the heart, and Peter may serve his cause: "Feed my lambs." A second time Christ asks, "Simon, son of John, do you love me?" A second time Peter replies, "Lord, you know that I'm your friend." Now notice. Jesus asks a third time: "Simon, son of John, are you my friend? Is even this much true? Do you really mean it?" Peter replies with a sob in his voice, "Lord, you know everything, you know that I'm your friend."

William Temple wrote of this passage: "There is no one of us here who, if he is honest, and knows what that word means, will answer, 'Yes, Lord, I love thee.' But we must be able to say, 'I am thy friend.' That will be enough. He will ask us in order that we may be sure that we do stand on his side, that we mean to give him our loyalty, and that our failures when they come, as of course they will, shall be failures of weakness and not the failures of traitors."

> "Lord, it is my chief complaint
> That my love is weak and faint;
> Yet I love Thee, and adore:
> O for grace to love Thee more."

Still, Peter's questions have not all been answered. Indeed, the Lord tells him only enough so that he may know the cost of discipleship. Peter receives marching orders instead of blue-prints: "Follow me."

Peter sees John following also, and asks, "Lord, what about this man?" All Peter's old curiosity has returned, and his questions are already beginning to crowd out the question of his Lord. That is why Jesus rather abruptly replies: "What is that to you? Your path is plain. Follow me."

We are so easily distracted in our devotion — even at Communion. But our Lord knows what we need most. Thomas a Kempis paraphrases the answer of Christ beautifully in his *Imitation of Christ:* "My son, be not curious, nor trouble thyself with idle anxieties, what is this or that to thee? Follow thou me. For what is this or that to thee, whether that man be such or such, or whether this man do or speak this or that? Thou shalt not need to answer for others. Thou shalt give account for thyself."

Let us take this to heart. In the Communion we do not find all the answers to all our questions, but we find our Lord. "I know whom I have believed" — and that is enough.

> "I know not how that Calvary's cross
> A world from sin could free;
> I only know its matchless love
> Has brought God's love to me."

The reality of this Supper does not depend upon whether I have found answers to all my questions. It depends upon one thing only — whether I have heard and answered his question: "Simon, son of John, do you love me?"

Well, do I? After all, I know that he loves me. That is why he has met me. The only question that remains is, Do I love him? And as I answer, I hear him say, "Follow me."